GREEN CHRISTIANITY

GREEN CHRISTIANITY

FIVE WAYS TO A SUSTAINABLE FUTURE

MARK I. WALLACE

Fortress Press

Minneapolis

GREEN CHRISTIANITY
Five Ways to a Sustainable Future

Cover design: Paul Boenke
Interior design and composition: PerfecType, Nashville, TN

Library of Congress Cataloging-in-Publication Data

Wallace, Mark I., 1956-
  Green Christianity : five ways to a sustainable future / Mark I. Wallace.
     p. cm.
  Includes index.
  ISBN 978-0-8006-6461-9 (alk. paper)
  1. Ecotheology. 2. Human ecology--Religious aspects--Christianity. 3. Nature--Religious aspects--Christianity. I. Title.
  BT695.5.W346 2010
  261.8'8--dc22
                                        2010016029

The paper used in this publication meets the minimum requirements of American National Standard for Information Sciences—Permanence of Paper for Printed Library Materials, ANSI Z329.48-1984.

Manufactured in the U.S.A.

14 13 12 11 10 1 2 3 4 5 6 7 8 9 10

TO KATIE AND CHRIS

CONTENTS

PREFACE

This book is an exercise in Earth-centered, body-loving Christian faith. Faith that values God in all things—every animal, rock, tree, body of water, and airy atmosphere that makes up life on Earth—is faith that takes joy in the delights of bodily pleasure within human community as well. The book will oscillate between celebration of the good creation God has made and exulting in the pleasures of the flesh that characterize intimate, sexual relations between persons. In turn, it will suggest that failure to love and pleasure the body has blunted the ability of people of faith to experience their organic kinship with the wider biotic order, thereby undercutting the spiritual basis of many persons' attempts to live sustainably in Earth community.

The book is divided into six chapters. Chapters 1 through 5 each offers a model for Earth- and body-affirming living based on spiritual values, while chapter 6 is a commentary on the documentary film *Renewal*, which celebrates the emerging religious environmental movement. An introduction to and exerpts from this important film come with the book. *Green Christianity's* core chapters provide five ways to a sustainable future and conclude with an analysis of the film's visually powerful case studies of practical green living.

While not obvious at first glance, Christianity, at its core, has always been a fleshly, earthly, material religion. Everyday, bodily existence—food and drink, life and death, humans and animals, land and sky—is recalled in countless rituals and stories as the primary medium through which God relates to humankind and the wider Earth community. Christianity's central ritual is a group meal that remembers the saving death of Jesus by celebrating the good gifts of creation—eating bread and drinking wine. Its central symbol is a cross made out of wood—two pieces of lumber lashed together as the means and site of Jesus' crucifixion. Its central belief focuses on the body—namely, that God became flesh in Jesus and thereby becomes one of us, a mortal, breathing life-form who experiences the joy and suffering of life on Earth. And Christianity's primary sacred document, the Bible, is suffused with rich, ecological imagery that stretches from the Cosmic Potter in Genesis who fashions Adam from the dust of the ground to the river of life in Revelation that flows from the throne of God, bright as crystal, vivifying the tree of life that yields its fruit to all of Earth's inhabitants. Christianity has long been a religion that invests the natural world with sacred meaning.

Christianity is also a religion that privileges amatory relationships, even though many people of faith have been trained to live the spiritual life drained of any erotic charge. Sexless, bloodless, humorless, divorced from all things fleshy and visceral—the life of faith often has been seen as a pitched battle between God's ways and human lust, the divine order and the lower order of base instincts, the heavenly world of bodiless bliss and this world of earthly drives and passions.

The Bible—or its interpretations—has much to do with this ugly division. Traditions of biblical reading that ignore, or make war against, Earth-based and body-loving religion have contributed greatly to some Christians' unease with locating physical pleasure on a spiritual foundation. Indeed, particular stories about the excesses of sexual license have been isolated to form an anti-sexual, anti-body template that shapes and deforms contemporary religious experience. The evils of unchecked sexual desire are purportedly illustrated in Adam and Eve's recognition of their nakedness and sexuality in the garden after they have sinned; Potiphar's wife, who tries to seduce Jacob and then accuses him of rape; Queen Jezebel, stereotyped as a heavily made-up seductress, who manipulated the men around her; and Salome, who danced lasciviously before Herod and persuaded him to offer her whatever she wanted, which turned out to be the head of John the Baptist.

The irony, however, is that the Bible is suffused with stories about the warmth and beauty of sexual intimacy that move beyond these narratives' prohibitions against lust and seduction. Consider the following accounts of love and affection that run like a red thread throughout the biblical story, challenging the common notion that religion and erotic pleasure are a contradiction in terms.

In Genesis, Rebekah sees Isaac in the fields of the Negev one evening. She is intrigued by his presence. "Who is the man over there," she asks Isaac's servant, "walking in the field to meet us?" (24:65). When the servant tells Isaac of Rebekah's interests, "then Isaac brought her into his mother Sarah's tent. He took Rebekah, and she became his wife; and he loved her. So Isaac was comforted after his mother's death" (24:67). In the beginning, the narrative of Isaac and Rebekah is a love story of heart-warming longing and tenderness.

The Song of Solomon is a lyric poem between two lovers sated with lush erotic imagery. It begins in a gushing torrent of desire, "Let him kiss me with the kisses of his mouth! For your love is better than wine!" (1:2), continues with impassioned descriptions of the beloved's body, "Your rounded thighs are like jewels, the work of a master hand; your two breasts are like two fawns, and the scent of your breath like apples" (7:1,3), and ends on a meditative note about the all-consuming power of love and romance, "Many waters cannot quench love, neither can floods drown it. If one offered for love all the wealth of one's house, it would be utterly scorned" (8:7). Rich, amorous relations between lovers is God's ideal of human fulfillment.

In the New Testament, Jesus' first miracle in the Gospel of John is changing water into wine at the wedding in Cana. When the wine ordered for the wedding runs out, Jesus transformed the contents of six large stone jars into an excellent *vino*. The wine steward then commended the bridegroom for his good taste: "Everyone serves the good wine first, and then the inferior wine after the guests have become drunk. But you have kept the good wine until now" (2:10). Following this story, Jesus is called a bridegroom in John, and in the other gospels he self-identifies as such (e.g., Luke 5:33-39), and claims his mission is to come into the world "eating and drinking" (Luke 7:34), in order to rebut the criticism that he is not fasting enough and takes too much pleasure in life. At the inauguration of his public ministry, Jesus blesses a marriage ceremony, celebrates God's good gifts of wine and food for human enjoyment, and names himself the groom (and by implication, the chef) in the gustatory, conjugal festival of loving relations between part-ners, family, and friends he seeks to lead.

The Johannine wedding miracle can be paired with another narrative about Jesus and amorous desire, the story of the unnamed woman who wets Jesus' feet with her tears and hair in the home of Simon the Pharisee in Luke 7. "And a woman in the city . . . stood behind [Jesus] at his feet, weeping, began to bathe his feet with her tears and to dry them with her hair. Then she continued kissing his feet, and anointed them with ointment" (vs. 37-38). At this point, Jesus senses Simon's dis-approval of this action, and says to him, "You did not anoint my head with oil, but she has anointed my feet with ointment. Therefore, I tell you, her sins, which are many, are forgiven, hence she has known great love" (vs. 46-47). Jesus luxuriates in this woman's touch. She comes to his feet—in the Bible, as we will see in chapter 3, feet is code language for genitals— and lovingly soaks them with her tears and wipes them with her hair. This transgressive act of brazen devotion stirs Jesus to rebuke his dinner host by publicly enjoying the kissing woman's lavish ardor.

Soul versus body, mind over matter, chastity against lust— the Bible has been read, wrongly, in my judgment, as under-girding the time-honored hierarchy that pits God and purity over and against sex and shame. But these stories of longing and desire—stories of holy lust, as it were—remind the faithful that sexual expression is one of the many gifts bestowed on the human family that binds us to the Earth and one another in mutual joy and soulful, heartfelt yearning.

The central claim of this book is that religion has a special role to play in saving the planet and loving the body. Religion, uniquely, has the power to fire the imagination and empower the will to nurture everyday sensual life. The embodiment crisis—the crisis of unsustainable living on Earth rooted in contempt of our bodies—is a crisis not of the *head,* but of the *heart.* The problem is not that we do not know how to stop climate change or love our flesh again, but rather that we lack the inner desire to redirect our culture toward a sustainable, body-affirming future. This book is a call to hope, not despair—a call for readers to discover meaning and purpose in their lives through a spiritually charged commitment to saving the Earth and loving themselves. Green desire for a verdant planet and bodily well-being are now possible because all things are envisioned as the enfleshment of God in the world around us.

The book is centered around an argument for "Christian animism"—the biblically inspired belief that all of creation is "animated" by God's presence—as the baseline conviction necessary for doing theology in an age of climate change in particular and contempt for the body in general. Insofar as Christianity, at times, has stood for belief in a sky-God far removed from earthly concerns, at first glance it may appear that classical Christianity and the animist world-view of first peoples who regarded all things as "ensouled" with sacred presence are polar opposites. In the main, however, Christian faith offers its practitioners a profound vision of God's this-worldly identity. By taking up the "green Jesus" and the "carnal Spirit" traditions within the biblical witness, I will show, scripturally speaking, that all things are bearers of divinity—the whole biosphere is filled with God's animating power—insofar as God signaled God's love for creation by incarnating Godself in Jesus and giving the Holy Spirit to indwell everything that exists on the planet. The miracle of Jesus as the living enfleshment of God in our midst—a miracle that is alongside the gift of the Spirit to the world since time immemorial—signals the ongoing vitality of God's sustaining presence within the natural order. God is not a sky-God divorced from the material world. As once God became earthly at the beginning of creation, and as once God became human in the body of Jesus, so now God continually enfleshes Godself through the Spirit in the embodied reality of life on Earth—including the many sensual pleasures of the flesh that accompany earthly life.

The Christian doctrines of creation, incarnation, and Spirit, therefore, are the seedbed of my Christian animist vision of the sacred character of the natural order. From this living source, all that exists is alive, all that exists is good, all that exists is holy. We will not save what we do not love, and unless, as a culture, we learn to love and care for the gift of the created order again, the prospects of saving the planet, and thereby ourselves as well, are terrifyingly bleak. But insofar as God is in everything and all things are interanimated by divine power and compassion, we will be on fire to fight against the specters of global warming and the accompanying loss of biodiversity as the great threats of our time.

As the bedrock religious tradition in Western culture, Christianity is essential to converting Americans' consumer-oriented lifestyles toward responsible Earth stewardship. Large-scale change is difficult, but change is possible. Many of the great social movements in American history—from the abolitionist movement in the nineteenth century to the civil rights movement in the twentieth—have been ignited by the moral vision of prophetic Christians. In turn, the green movement of the twenty-first century will only become successful when churches everywhere make sustainable living and body-centered values essential to their identity and mission. The day is coming when it will become as morally unthinkable for Christians to drive a gas-guzzling car or use inefficient standard light bulbs as it is for Christians today to own slaves or insist that women be denied the right to vote. Like these previous seismic shifts in Christianity's moral topography, the green movement as a *religious* revolution is beginning to take shape as well.

Thomas Friedman writes that "green is the new red, white, and blue." Crossing over the political divide that separates red state and blue state Christians, the new green Christianity brings together opposing parties into a common commitment to Earth-centered religious practice and civic engagement. Here I articulate again what I take to be the central claim of Christianity—namely, that God incarnates Godself in human flesh—which means that God exists in and through the planet, that Earth itself is divinely inspir(it)ed. The Earth, in a word, is *sacred*. Rediscovering the natural world and our bodies as holy ground is the baseline conviction that will sustain the long struggle by people of faith to build a livable, verdant, and durable world that future generations can enjoy.

In this way I hope to challenge some critics' assumptions that religion is a strictly personal issue and thereby irrelevant, or even hostile, to community-based goods. Since the Enlightenment, religion's cultured critics insist that faith is a sectarian, private matter unrelated to public life. And since 9/11, the cry by religion's detractors is that "religion kills." My case is that spiritually grounded environmental beliefs and practices are a positive social force because they encourage citizens to subordinate private concerns to larger goods. Such beliefs and practices have the potential to revive both Christian experience and liberal societies at a time when civic life is characterized by cynicism and despair. Indeed, my hope in writing this book is to demonstrate how religious faith—now wedded to the green movement—can stimulate wider public commitments to sustainable living and democratic renewal at a time when global environmental deterioration is threatening the future of our planet.

Chapter One

FIND GOD EVERYWHERE

"But ask the animals, and they will teach you;
the birds of the air, and they will tell you; ask the
plants of the earth, and they will teach you; and
the fish of the sea will declare to you." Job 12:7-8

Christian Animism

One morning, during a recent sabbatical in Costa Rica, my family and I sought a viewing of a quetzal in its natural habitat in the Monteverde Cloudforest Preserve. The quetzal is arguably the most beautiful bird in Central America. It is covered with shiny, metallic green feathers, bright red breast, and long streamers for its tail. Its glorious train is so long that when the male quetzal leaves its perch it often flies backward for a moment to avoid damaging its sweeping tail feathers. With the help of a guide, we found a female quetzal in the forest working on preparing a nest in the decaying trunk of an old tree. Often aflight in the forest canopy, this resplendent creature had traveled down to the understory to make her nest. Glittering in the filtered light, the quetzal bounced from the tree trunk to a limb overhead while making a whining, plaintive song. Her call sounded like the yelp of a newborn puppy, yearning and soulful. We watched and listened to the quetzal for a long while until she sallied forth through the damp forest. I resonated deeply to the longing in the quetzal's song, and I wondered, Am I hearing God somehow in this mournful cry? In the haunting call of this bird, is God speaking to me as well, imploring me to open myself again to the beauty of creation— a beauty so movingly evoked by the quetzal's melody in the early morning of this montane forest? In the refrain of a Native American prayer,

> Beauty is before me
> And beauty is behind me
> Above and below me hovers the beautiful
> I am surrounded by it
> I am immersed in it
> In my youth I am aware of it
> And in old age I shall walk quietly
> The beautiful trail.[1]

For me, the beautiful trail—the natural world—serves as the primary site for the sort of spiritual encounters observing the queztal provided. Church sanctuaries and meditation rooms continue to be settings where such encounters take place, but I need to be outdoors or in a worship space that tracks the rhythms of the natural world in order to be brought short and rendered expectant of a visit from another reality. "I enter a swamp as a sacred place—a *sanctum sanctorum*," wrote Henry David Thoreau.² The whoosh of a strong wind, the taste of the salty sea on my tongue, the graceful movement of a monarch butterfly, the arc of the bright sky on a cold winter night, the screech of a red-tailed hawk—these events are preternatural overtures that greet me from another plane of existence. It is not that this other plane stands over and against everyday reality, but rather that commonplace existence is a window into another world that is *this* world but now experienced in its pregnant depths and always-already-there possibilities. Daily, embodied life is an icon through which the supersensible world is encountered in the here-and-now. Life is twofold. Like the disciples on the road to Emmaus in Luke's Gospel, who walked and talked with Jesus but did not recognize him until their understanding was changed—like the gift of bread and wine that is not experienced as God's body and blood apart from its ritual transformation—the natural world stands mute until it is spiritually encountered as saturated with grace and meaning. In secular parlance, to be human is to dwell poetically on the Earth; in religious terms, to be human is to dwell mythically on the Earth.³ How to experience Earth mythico-poetically—how to find God through the daily miracle of ordinary existence—is the primary thrust of this book.

In the fourth century C.E., the theologian Eusebius wrote a massive multi-volume work titled *The Evangelical Preparation.* He argued that the pre-Christian Greek philosophers paved the way for the arrival of the Christian message. According to Eusebius, the writers of antiquity possessed an inchoate and rudimentary understanding of the nature of human longing for divinity that later Christian authors fully developed through the teachings of the New Testament. Today, nature is my evangelical preparation for hearing the Gospel anew and afresh; it is the ground on which the biblical message makes meaning. Without the experience of creation as sacred place, the Christian story rings hollow and lacks the necessary resonance for my full comprehension of its power and scope. Long walks along the shoreline or sitting meditation in the woods opens me to the arrival of God's presence in a fashion that is always new and replete with unforeseen energy and opportunities.

The basic orientation that drives my appreciation of nature as fertile ground for receiving the Gospel teaching is what I call "Christian animism"—the biblically inflected conviction that all creation is infused with, or "animated," by God's presence. The term *animism* has its origins in the early academic study of the vernacular belief-systems of indigenous peoples in Africa and the Americas. It originated with nineteenth century British anthropologist E. B. Tylor, who used it to describe how primordial people attributed "life" or "soul" to all things, living and nonliving. Sharing resonances with the Latin word *animus*, which means soul or spirit, among other definitions, animism came to stand for the orienting worldview of indigenous communities that nonhuman nature is "ensouled" or "inspirited" with sacred presence and power. As Graham Harvey writes, animism

> is typically applied to religions that engage with a wide community of living beings with whom humans share this world or particular locations within it. It might be summed up by the phrase "all that exists lives" and, sometimes, the additional understanding that "all that lives is holy." As such the term *animism* is sometimes applied to

particular indigenous religions in comparison to Christianity or Islam, for example.[4]

What intrigues me about Harvey's definition is his assumption that monotheistic traditions such as Christianity should be regarded as distinct from animism. Initially this makes sense in light of the historic Christian proclivity to cast aspersions on the material world and the flesh as inferior to the concerns of the soul. Pseudo-Titus, for example, in an extra-canonical exhortation to Christian asceticism from late antiquity, urges its readers to cleanse themselves of worldly pollution by overcoming fleshly temptations: "Blessed are those who have not polluted their flesh by craving for this world, but are dead to the world that they may live for God!"[5] At first glance, Christianity's emphasis on making room for God by denying the world and the flesh is at odds with the classical animist belief in the living goodness of all inhabitants of sacred Earth.

In the main, however, Christian faith offers its practitioners a profound vision of God's this-worldly identity. Harvey's presumption that Christianity and animism are distinct from one another is at odds with the biblical worldview that all things are bearers of divinity—the whole biosphere is filled with God's animating power—insofar as God signaled God's love for creation by incarnating Godself in Jesus and giving the Holy Spirit to indwell everything that exists on the planet. The miracle of Jesus as the living enfleshment of God in our midst—a miracle that is alongside the gift of the Spirit to the world since time immemorial—signals the ongoing vitality of God's sustaining presence within the natural order. God is not a sky-God divorced from the material world. As once God became earthly at the beginning of creation, and as once God became human in the body of Jesus, so now God continually enfleshes Godself through the Spirit in the embodied reality of life on earth.

For many people, however, to identify Christianity as an animist religion is an odd connection to make. To make this identification, I am suggesting that the incarnational enfleshment of God in Jesus, and the biblical promise of the Spirit to indwell everything that exists, are the paradigmatic expressions of God's presence in all things throughout the created order. Christian animism, in a nutshell, is the conviction that everything God made is a bearer of the Holy Spirit. It is important to note, however, that Christian animism is not equivalent to other similar-sounding perspectives that are often equated or used interchangeably with the term *animism* in daily discourse. *Paganism* and *heathenism*, Latin and old English terms, respectively, stand for the *paganus* or country-dwelling people, and the "heathen" or people of the heath, both of which developed agricultural spiritualities of sacrifice and planting-and-harvest rituals prior to the arrival of Christianity in Western cultures. *Pantheism*, on the other hand, emphasizes that God and the cosmos are one and the same reality without remainder. Animism—now refracted though biblical optics—shares affinities with these viewpoints, but emphasizes with more force the indwelling of *Spirit* in all things—echoing its Latin root's notion of "soul" or "spirit"—so that the great expanse of the natural world can be re-envisioned as sacred and thereby deserving of our nurture and love.

Of the current models of the interconnected relation between God and Earth, *panentheism* is closest to Christian animism. Panentheist theologian Sallie McFague argues for the mutual, internal relatedness of God and creation but notes that God is not *fully* realized in the material world; God is *in* the world, indeed, but God is not "totally" embodied within everyday existence. She says:

> Pantheism says that God is embodied, necessarily and totally; traditional theism claims that God is disembodied, necessarily and totally; panentheism suggests that God is embodied but not necessarily or totally. Rather, God is sacramentally embodied: God is mediated, expressed, in and through embodiment, but not necessarily or totally.[6]

While my sensibility and McFague's are deeply aligned, my Christian animism pushes her initial point further by suggesting that God is *fully* and *completely* embodied within the natural world. Here the emphasis does not fall on the limited relatedness of God and world such that God, finally, can escape the world. Rather the focus falls on the world as *thoroughly embodying* God's presence. Unlike many Christian theologies which emphasize God's *transcendence*, my position, akin to McFague's, champions divine *subscendence:* God flowing out into the Earth, God becoming one of us in Jesus, God gifting to all creation the Spirit to infuse all things with divine energy and love. Now nothing is held back as God overflows Godself into the bounty of the natural world. Now all things are bearers of the sacred; everything that *is* is holy; each and every creature is a portrait of God.

This fully earthen enfleshment of God in nature hearkens back to language from the fourth of the seven great ecumenical councils of formative Christianity that continue to define the basic beliefs of Orthodox, Catholic, and Protestant Christians today. In 451 C.E., the ecumenical churches met in Chalcedon, in what is today Western Turkey, to formulate a new under-standing of how the divine and the human relate in Jesus of Nazareth. The historic churches decided that in the one per-son of Jesus, divinity and humanity are fully realized in an organic and permanent unity that admits no separation or con-fusion. The Chalcedonian Creed asks all Christians to confess to the "one and the same Christ, Son, Lord, Only-begotten, to be acknowledged in two natures without confusion, altera-tion, division, separation; the distinction of natures being by no means taken away by the union, but rather the property of each nature being preserved."[7] Jesus' two natures—divine and human—come together in one personal life. Completely human and fully divine, the one whole person of Jesus of Nazareth is both a human being like the rest of humankind and, at the same time, the incarnation of God.

It is Chalcedonian Christianity's theological grammar, so to speak, that shapes my model of how God and the Earth are inseparably unified. Without separation or confusion, God is fully embodied in creation, on the one hand, and God is still God, on the other. As Jesus is fully divine and fully human, so also is God fully God and fully infused within the lifeweb of our planetary existence. Like the union of divinity and human-ity in Jesus, the natural world, while distinct from God with its own identity and integrity, is nevertheless fully interpenetrated by divine life. Creation, then, is God completely realizing God-self in carnal space in the same way that God fully realized Godself in the birth of Jesus. Jesus is the integrated person who unifies divinity and humanity; Earth is the ground that brings together material existence and God's presence in unity and love. Or to phrase this point differently, as God's Spirit *ensouls* all things with sacred purpose, so also are all things the *enfleshment* of divine power and compassion on Earth. This dialectic of ensoulment (Earth is blessed as the living realization of divine grace) and enfleshment (God pours out Godself into the carnal reality of lived existence) is the mainspring of my Christian animist vision of reality.

The biblical ideas of creation, incarnation, and Spirit are the fountainhead of the Christian animist vision of the sacred character of the natural order. From this living source, to paraphrase Harvey, all that exists is alive, all that exists is good, all that exists is holy. We will not save what we do not love, and unless, as a culture, we learn to love and care for the gift of the created order again, the prospects of saving the planet, and thereby ourselves as well, are terrifyingly bleak. But insofar as God is in everything, and all things are inter-animated by divine power and concern, we can affirm that God is carnal, God is earthen, God is flesh. And with this animist affirmation, the will is empowered, and the imagination ignited, to fight against the specters of global warming and the loss of biodiversity as the great threats of our time.

Hungry for eruptions of the animist sacred, personally speaking, I mourn in our time the continued loss of the wider community of nature as the seed bed for full fruitions of God in my life. Selfishly, I don't want the natural world to suffer further degradation because I do not want God to die for me. For me, climate change and the loss of natural habitats mean that God's presence in the world is weakened and diminished as well. It is not that God is completely absent from me during this period of eco-squalor, but rather, as Martin Buber said about God in the death camps, I experience God in eclipse—I experience God being driven into hiding by laying waste to our common home.[8] The burden of faith today is to maintain the seemingly impossible contradiction between faith in God's earthen reality against the realization that Spirit is in retreat due to our continual assaults on God's fleshy presence.

In every respect, therefore, the Earth crisis is a spiritual crisis because without a vital, fertile planet it will be difficult to find traces of divine wonder and providence in the everyday order of things. When the final arctic habitat for the polar bear melts into the sea due to human-induced climate change, I will lose something of God's beauty and power in my life. When the teeming swell of equatorial amphibians can no longer adapt to deforestation and rising global temperatures, something of God will disappear as well, I fear. I am like the first peoples of the Americas who experienced the sacred within the Black Hills of what is now South Dakota, or on top of Mount Graham in southern Arizona, and then found that when these places were degraded, something of God was missing as well. Without these and other places charged with sacred power, I am lost on the Earth. Without still-preserved landed sites saturated with divine presence, I am a wanderer with no direction, a person without hope, a believer experiencing the death of God on a planet suffering daily from human greed and avarice.

Global Warming

If the current scientific consensus about climate change is accurate, then we are now living in an objectively apocalyptic situation in which our planet is teetering on the edge of disaster. Jim Hansen, top climate specialist at NASA, claims we have just ten years to reduce greenhouse gases before global warming reaches an unstoppable tipping point and transforms our natural world into a "totally different planet."[9] Global warming—the trapping in Earth's atmosphere of greenhouse gases such as CO^2 from car and power plant emissions—is causing air and ocean temperatures to rise catastrophically to new levels.

The specter of rising temperatures has recently been documented by the Intergovernmental Panel on Climate Change, a UN-sponsored group consisting of dozens of climate scientists from more than one hundred countries.[10] While Earth's temperature rose by one degree last century, the panel's current predictions are that global temperatures will rise by three to ten degrees this century, resulting in the widespread melting of Arctic sea ice, mountain glaciers, and perhaps even the Greenland landmass. This mass melting could then raise sea levels, astonishingly, by one or two feet, or more, causing low-lying shore communities such as the San Francisco Bay Area and lower Manhattan to gradually disappear. Whole island chains, such as the Maldives off the coast of India, or the much-loved Venice, Italy, would eventually slip under water. Even now, climate change is contributing to a global die-off of species similar to the last mass extinction event over 65 million years ago when the great dinosaurs were wiped out. Today, biologists conservatively estimate that 30,000 plant and animal species per year are driven to extinction—even the polar bear is now proposed as a threatened species.[11]

While science can analyze the record climate change since the industrial revolution—for example, that eleven of the last twelve years rank among the twelve warmest years of global temperature since 1850—it cannot provide the necessary moral foundation for answering the existential question—What difference does it make whether our children or grandchildren survive the killer weather that our collective carbon dumping is destined to cause? Why care about future generations at all? In the words of the famous Schlitz beer ad of my youth, "You only go around once in life, so grab for all the gusto you can get!" Why not maximize one's individual pleasure and stop worrying about possible consequences? Science cannot answer this question; only religion, or a value-system centered on higher goods, can provide this answer. While many scientists themselves are motivated by moral and even religious concerns, science cannot say—as the religions of Abraham claim—that the natural world is God's creation, intricately designed for the sustenance and joy of all beings, and therefore humans are called upon to restrain their appetites in order to love and care for their planet home. In particular, science cannot assert, as religion can, that the Earth is *sacred* and therefore deserving of our protection. My assertion is that without such an all-encompassing, hyper-moral claim, the prospects for saving the planet are slim indeed. It is for this reason that I have written this book about Christianity and the rush to save the planet—to reshape our attitudes of indifference to the natural world by recovering the core biblical conviction that Earth is holy ground deserving of our love and protection.

In the face of this global crisis, therefore, science is not enough. Like our chronic smoking behavior from a previous generation, we now know that our consumer-oriented, carbon-intensive lifestyles are killing us—and many other species as well—but we cannot stop our behavior. We are falling-down carbon drunks, fossil fuel addicts who cannot break our collective addiction cycle. Only religion—or some alternative religion-like moral system with global interests—can save us now. Only religion—or some other overarching belief-system committed to the health of all living things—has the moral authority and symbolic potency to break our shared carbon addiction cycle by motivating us to look beyond our private self-interest and to the greater good of the planet itself.[12]

It's not international terrorism, but global warming that is the most dangerous security threat to civilization as we know it. Yet, otherwise powerful nations seem impotent to stop the coming cataclysm. So, in the face of chronic political dysfunction, religious congregations are rising up to confront the challenge. These communities of faith have the power to gather the fragments of human vision for a just and sustainable world into a coherent moral narrative that can enable the type of revolutionary social change needed in this historical moment. Precisely at this point in our history when the Earth is most under siege, people of faith have become acutely aware of the ancient ecological wisdom at the roots of their religious traditions that can motivate the lifestyle and public policy changes necessary for saving the Earth. Religious communities are waking up to the tasks of climate rescue and planetary justice in our time.

While I will allude to different religions in this book, I primarily want to analyze how Christianity is awakening to its responsibility to fight global warming and save the planet. No longer relegated to a long list of special interests, today care for creation has become a core moral issue for biblically centered Christians concerned about climate change and the loss of global biodiversity. This newly embraced passion for the well-being of the natural world is provoking a seismic shift in values within American culture and politics. One of the reasons that Barack Obama won the 2008 U.S. presidential election is that the electorate was dismayed over the Republican Party's and former President Bush's failure, among other issues, to break America's dependence on fossil fuels by developing a sustainable energy policy that could blunt the impact of climate change. Oddly, George W. Bush seemed both aware of the problem and helpless to stop it. "America is addicted to oil," Mr. Bush exclaimed in his 2006 State of the Union address, calling for new but vague forms of energy independence. However, this hazy call for a different energy policy was belied by the former president's cozy relations with Big Oil, his opposition to anti-pollution enforcement, and his ongoing receipt of tens of million of dollars in oil and gas donations during the time of his Texas governorship and U.S. presidency. Witnessing the president lecture American citizens about the country's dependency on fossil fuels ("America is addicted to oil") was like watching a recovering drunk opine about responsible drinking—hypocrisy of this sort renders such calls to change suspicious at best.

As he struggled to articulate a sound and sustainable energy policy, George W. Bush's evangelical Christian base began to crack early in his second term over which priorities should govern the conservative movement in coming years.[13] The stress was due in part to conflicting attitudes about the nature of the biblically predicted "end times" and how Christians, and the politicians they support, should make policy in light of Christ's supposed imminent return to Earth in judgment. Some traditional Christians promulgate a belief in Dispensationalism that views the planet as dispensable within God's master plan—the belief that God has ordained history to unfold according to divinely prescribed ages or "dispensations" in which the final age, the end times, will be ushered in by Jesus' return, the rapture of true Christians, and the firey destruction of the Earth.[14] But many Christians, including many evangelicals, reject this sort of Dispensationalist apocalypticism in favor of a return to the biblical ideal of creation care: restoring Earth as a garden of beauty blessed by God and tended by God's special caretakers—us—the human community. As conservative activist Matthew Sleeth writes:

> I am convinced that when the church becomes fully engaged in the problems of creation care, we will overcome seemingly insurmountable odds. As the thirty million evangelical Christians—and all those who consider themselves people of faith—grow in their understanding that God holds us accountable for care of his creation, we will begin to see positive changes on an unprecedented scale.[15]

Indeed, a recent article in the *New York Times Magazine* featured interviews of so-called "green evangelicals" who now see a "biblical mandate for government action to stop global warming."[16] And a just-released national survey indicates that 35 percent of U.S. religious conservatives identify protecting the environment as a top priority.[17] Moving beyond polarizing social issues, such as homosexuality, abortion, and stem-cell research, churches on the left *and* the right are articulating a Christian response to global warming by promoting renewable energy, community-based agriculture, and conservation of natural resources. This book, then, consists of both analysis *of* this change and advocacy *for* this change—a call to move beyond the impasse between *red* state and *blue* state politics by embracing the power of *green* religion to engender civic renewal and environmental health in our time.

The Greening of the Churches

The specter of global warming and ecological depredation haunt the contemporary landscape. But, practically speaking, what hands-on activities are Christian and other congregations doing to promote climate recovery and environmental justice? Today, many North American churches, synagogues, mosques, and other places of worship are transforming themselves into forward-based earth-care centers committed to protecting God's creation, sustainable lifestyles, and safeguarding the public health.[18] In the wider Christian community, powerful new voices for change and hope are emerging. The mission of the states-based Interfaith Power and Light is to blunt the impact of global warming by helping churches conserve energy resources; the IPL provides free energy audits, alternative power advice, and green building upgrades for religious centers seeking to overcome their reliance on nonrenewable energy. The National Religious Partnership for the Environment publishes green educational curricula for the major branches of the Catholic, Protestant, and Jewish faiths; it also brings together religious leaders, corporate heads, environmental activists, and scientists to strategize about how faith-based public policy focused on sustainability can blunt the impacts of climate change. The Evangelical Environmental Network, in part, emerged from the 2002 "What Would Jesus Drive?" campaign that linked transportation choices with following Jesus. Causing splits within the Republican evangelical voting bloc, the EEN recently called for mandatory greenhouse gas emissions caps based on the biblical precept that Christians should be good stewards of creation. Finally, the Sierra Club and the National Council of Churches have joined forces to mobilize faith communities to stop drilling in Alaska and to promote clean water campaigns in the American Southwest. The Sierra Club's Faith Partnerships Program has created numerous faith-and-action cells to address immediate environmental problems and the long-term crisis of global warming.

Consider the following case study of a Protestant church in the upper Midwest as illustrative of the real changes that congregational environmental engagement can bring about in our time. This past fall I traveled to Frame Memorial Presbyterian Church in Stevens Point, Wisconsin, to both participate in and witness the church's ongoing transformation into a green congregation. To this end, Frame Memorial is regularly incorporating environmental stewardship teachings into worship and educational programs; developing an extensive recycling program for paper, cell phones, and eyeglasses, among other items; reducing their own consumption of nonrenewable forms of energy by converting their incandescent light bulbs to compact flourescents; and practicing good earth-keeping on their own grounds through the establishment of a native-plantings shade garden, the use of non-toxic cleaners and fertilizers, and the purchase of fair trade products. Frame Memorial's good example is spreading outward into the community. Church members employ Watts Up? meters to measure their electricity use in their homes. They have joined forces with a dozen other places of worship to form an Interfaith Community of the Earth to support other congregations' "green teams." They have partnered with the the municipality of Stevens Point to implement a sustainability systems approach in all aspects of town planning, from land use and wastewater treatment to green building design and alternative modes of transportation.

What I find most striking about Frame Memorial is the implementation of a series of "Season of Creation" services and sermons in the fall of each year. Pioneered by Norman Habel, the Season of Creation has recently emerged as a new season in the church year when different communities of life-forms—oceans, sky, soil, wetlands, animals, birds, trees—are celebrated as the power and presence of God in creation.[19] Pastor Susan Gilbert Zencka crafts six services in September and early October around the theme of the blessings of creation and our responsibilities towards its care and preservation. Not content with a once-a-year creation-based ritual or an occasional ecological service project, she has brought her passion for Earth community into the heart of the church's liturgical calendar, core worship experience, and evangelical mission. Her sermons are both lyrically playful and morally serious. She includes conversations between God and an angel about the virtues of native grasslands, musings about the meaning of storms and floods in our lives, and a paean to the wonder of coral reefs and a lament about their degradation through our dumping of carbon into the oceans. One such sermon, "The Web of Creation and Dollar Stores," is a powerful argument for the interconnectedness and inherent worth of all things. Building on her earlier sermon regarding the sacredness of wetlands, Zencka maintains that nothing within creation is a commodity per se because every biotic community is charged with sacred presence. All life is holy:

> So what we have learned about wetlands on our own reveals the same truth that we see in the Bible—God values even that which humans do not value. Each piece of creation is good, and it is all of value to the whole

of it. We are only beginning to understand how life is interwoven, and how the web of creation cannot be disassembled without damage. . . . All creation is charged with divine presence—this is the understanding woven through Scripture, which is generally known as panentheism: God in all things. This is not pantheism, that God is the same as all things, but panentheism, God is in all things. This does not mean that everything is the same, as in the dollar store—everything a dollar, no matter what it is. No, in God's economy, each thing has value in and of itself—they are not commodities for humans, everything is created, and has its own purpose. Light is good as light, water is good as water, earth is good, plants and animals and fish and birds are good, and humans too are good— there is intrinsic value to each thing in creation. . . . They have value in themselves, so we do not consume more than we need, we do not consume in a way that is unsustainable, we treat animals with respect and care, and we treat each other with respect and care.[20]

Perhaps some Christians will think Pastor Zencka has gone too far in her valorization of creation as holy ground. To envision nature as sacred—or to say, as Zencka does, that "all creation is charged with divine presence"—may appear to undercut God's role as the unique and absolute bearer of sacred worth in a world of diverse life forms that only have relative value in relation to God. Some may feel that only God is worthy of devotion and praise; only God has absolute value in a world of relative things. From this perspective, to venerate Earth community as sacred borders on the extreme of a type of paganism or idolatry that dare not speak its name.

It is instructive to contrast this potential criticism of Zencka's
earthen spirituality with a recent article in *E: The Environmental Magazine* entitled "The Scoop on Dirt: Why We Should
All Worship the Ground We Walk On."[21] The article argues
that soil, while generally unrecognized and taken for granted,
is essential to the wellbeing of life on Earth. Soil traps and
recharges rainwater for drinking purposes. It provides habitat
for numerous plants and animals. It recycles decaying organic
matter, which in turn becomes a source of new energy. And
soil functions as a giant carbon sink for trapping dangerous
carbon dioxide emissions that would otherwise escape into
the atmosphere. As Lester Brown puts it, "The thin layer of
topsoil covering the planet's land surface is the foundation
of civilization."[22] Unheralded and neglected, soil is worthy of
our respect, even our adoration and reverence, because it is
foundational to the life-sustaining ecosystems we rely on for
daily sustenance.

I find it ironic that the modern secular environmental movement is attaching sacred significance to soil and earth—that we
should, as it were, worship the ground we walk on—at the
same time that some Christians remain troubled by the ascription of holiness to anything other than God. God's demand
in the Torah that Israel should not worship the image of any
earthen lifeform, and Paul's similar denunciation in the New
Testament of idolaters who worship creatures rather than the
Creator, seem to cut off any return path back to a view of
God as fundamentally nature-centered and the Earth as holy
ground worthy of our reverence and devotion. But the strange
and wonderful biblical traditions of the green Jesus and the
carnal Spirit within Christian testimony do offer resources for
precisely this return route—a road less traveled, where Jesus

and Spirit are depicted as fully embodied in the Earth and the natural world itself is reenvisioned as sacred place.

The witness of Christian scripture and traditions is to the world as an abode of divinity, the home of life-giving Spirit, God's here-and-now dwelling place where the warp and woof of everyday life is sacred. God is not a dispassionate and distant potentate, as in classical feudal theology, who exercises dominion over the universe from some far-removed place. Rather, in and through this planet that is our common home, God, now grounded in the Earth, is earnestly working with us to heal the planet. It is not blasphemous, therefore, to say that nature is sacred. It is not mistaken to find God's presence in all things. To speak in the language of Christian animism, it is not wrong to reenvision Christianity as continuous with the worldviews of the first peoples who bore witness to and experienced divinity everywhere—who saw and felt the Spirit alive in every rock, tree, animal, and body of water they encountered. Christianity can now do the same, and Christians can say, "Sacred is the ground we stand on; holy is the land where we are planted; blessed is the Earth within which we live and move and have our being." Without this affirmation—without the hope and energy and long-term staying power this affirmation brings to communities of faith—our capacity to heal the planet's ability to sustain future generations is badly undermined.

"We are on the precipice of climate system tipping points beyond which there is no redemption," wrote Jim Hansen, director of the NASA Goddard Institute for Space Studies, in 2003. As we reach these catastrophic tipping points, what will human existence on Earth look like in ten or fifteen years from now? Chronic heat waves will provoke megadroughts and render daily life unbearable at times. Arctic permafrost and sea ice will crack and disappear, causing islands and shorelines to shrink and vanish. Continued carbon dumping will render the world's oceans more acidic and ultimately lethal to coral reefs and fish stocks. Melting permafrost in Siberia and elsewhere will release huge amounts of methane into the atmosphere, resulting in killer hurricanes and tsunamis. Biodiverse ecosystems will collapse and produce dead monocultures of invasive species, where the basic dynamic of plant pollination itself is undermined. And a hotter and less forgiving planet will cause crop failures and large stretches of arable land to become desert, mosquito-borne diseases such as dengue fever and malaria to reach epidemic proportions, and mass migrations of tens of millions of people as rising sea levels destroy homes and communities. In the near future, we will look back at greenhouse gas-induced events, such as the European heat wave of 2003 that killed 30,000 people or Hurricane Katrina in 2005—the costliest natural disaster in U.S. history that killed 1,800 people—as telltale portends of the coming storm. We will remember other positive environmental changes—the banning of DDT in the U.S. in the 1960s, the general eradication of ozone-depleting CFCs in the 1980s—and then wonder why we were not able to extricate ourselves from the Big Oil economy that was even then destroying the planet. In 2015, 2020, or 2025, we will rue the day that we allowed deniers of global warming to confuse the public into thinking that the current climate change is a natural cycle. We will recall the definitive reports by the Millennium Ecosystem Assessment in 2005, and the Intergovernmental Panel on Climate Change in 2007, based on tens of thousands of studies by hundreds of climate researchers over many years of investigation, which made clear to us that our fossil fuel economy is the most important factor driving the dangerous climate changes we now see all around us.

With an alarming sense of urgency, we will know then, even as we know now, that it is time to act.

Every generation, to borrow Thomas Berry's phrase, has its great work. Every generation has an overarching sense of responsibility for the welfare of the whole that gathers together people and societies across their cultural and ideological differences. In this generation, our great work will be to fight global warming by reenvisioning our relationship to Earth, not as exploiters but as biotic kinspeople with the myriad life-forms that populate our common home. This is the mandate of our time. As Berry writes,

> The Great Work before us, the task of moving modern industrial civilization from its present devastating influence on the Earth to a more benign mode of presence, is not a role that we have chosen. It is a role given to us, beyond any consultation with ourselves. We did not choose. We were chosen by some power beyond ourselves for this historical task. We did not choose the moment of our birth, who our parents will be, our particular culture or the historical moment when we will be born. . . . The nobility of our lives, however, depends upon the manner in which we come to understand and fulfill our assigned roles.[23]

Every generation has a sacred calling to seize the moment and battle the forces of oppression and degradation so that future generations can live richer and more meaningful lives. The great work of our generation will be to develop inspired models of sustainable development that promote ecological and climate justice for all of God's children. Sustainability is a proleptic, forward-looking category that focuses on the long-term viability of working organizational models, namely: How can institutions today secure and manage the labor and environmental resources necessary for achieving their economic goals while also preserving the capacity of future human communities and ecosystems to survive and flourish? Native American folklore often speaks of animal and related resource management practices done with an eye toward their impact on the seventh generation to come. Seventh-generation full-cost business and accounting practices relocate the goal of financial profitability within the context of fair labor performance, responsible consumption of energy, and careful management of waste.[24] Sustainable development, then, articulates policies that address this generation's vital needs without sacrificing the ability of future generations to meet their own vital needs. For highly industrialized economies like our own, sustainability will be predicated on kicking our habits of dependence on fossil fuels, the primary source of global climate change. This book will provide the theological and moral foundations for practical responses to weaning ourselves off unsustainable coal, oil, and natural gas supplies in order to save the planet for future generations.

Religious faith is uniquely suited to fire the imagination and empower the will to make the necessary changes that can break the cycle of addiction to nonrenewable energy. Many of the great social movements in this country's history—the abolitionist groundswell of the nineteenth century, the suffragist associations of the early twentieth century, and, most notably in recent history, the civil rights movement in the 1950s and

1960s—were energized by prophetic Christian leaders who brought together their scriptural values and passion for justice to animate a moral force for change more powerful than any other force to stop them. To paraphrase William James, religion today, in the face of cataclysmic climate change, must become the moral equivalent of war by becoming more disciplined, more resourceful, and more visionary in fighting the causes of global ecological depredation. The supreme calling of our time will be for all of us to find a spiritually grounded and morally compelling approach to engaging the problem of climate change—and to do so now, before it is too late.

Chapter Two

READ THE BIBLE WITH GREEN EYES

But we have this treasure in clay jars, so that it may be made clear that this extraordinary power belongs to God and does not come from us. We are afflicted in every way, but not crushed. . . . For while we live, we are always being given up to death for Jesus' sake, so that the life of Jesus may be visible in our mortal flesh. —2 Cor. 4:7-8, 11

The Earthen Bible

My hope is that this book will provide the moral and theological energy for a heartfelt and meaningful response to the crisis of ecological degradation in our time. For people of faith, this energy first circulates in the sacred texts that tell the stories of how ancient human communities came to inhabit and care for their natural environments. The biblical witness, for Christians, is the primary conduit of this energy. A living voice of hope and encouragement, scripture teaches that verdant, sustainable living is God's way in a world often indifferent to the joy and beauty of life in creation. The Earth is not dead matter, but a living being—in biblical terms, it is God's "creation"—and, as such, it is deserving of our love and protection.

In the epigraph to this chapter from 2 Corinthians, the apostle Paul writes that his broken, mortal body is a clay jar that shines forth the power of God to the early church in Corinth. Ironically, though Paul's flesh is riddled with suffering and pulsing toward death, it has become the vehicle that literally bodies forth the life-giving message of Christian witness. Paul's provocative trope of his body as a fractured clay pot through which the living power of the gospel is offered to others is the ground for my reimagining the Bible as a "clay jar," as it were, through which the liberating message of Jesus' life and death is poured into the world. Like Paul's body, the Bible is a humanly conceived, clay jar; it is the mortal, fleshy, suffering means by which God's healing power is communicated to the wider community.

With this Earth-based scriptural image in mind, we now see that something extraordinary is happening today in biblical interpretation: the Bible, the clay jar of our time, is being read from an ecological perspective (that is, from an Earth-centered or "earthen" perspective) in which the wider natural world is regarded as an active agent and center of value essential to a full-bodied understanding of the sacred texts. While the hints of a more encompassing environmental message have always been obvious to even a cursory reader of the Bible—consider, for example, the indispensable role of creation in Genesis and the Psalms or the crucial importance of the incarnation of Jesus in the Gospels—most theologians have generally subordinated the Bible's Earth-centered themes to the message of redemption focused on human persons. Traditionally, Earth functioned as the background to the main sweep of the biblical story, which, at least in historic Christian thought, was classically understood as the message of personal salvation for the individual human subject. The natural world was relegated to the role of a bit player in the drama of human redemption. This classical "personalist" Bible is now in tension with the emerging "earthen" Bible. Like Paul's suffering flesh, the Bible's substantive teachings about the Earth and its inhabitants are currently regarded as constitutive of the Gospel message rather than as a backdrop to its supposedly primary emphasis on overcoming "this world" in favor of the "world to come." Assigning long-neglected significance to the sacred Earth and all of its members, human and nonhuman, as the true *subjects* of the biblical narrative moves, as Norman Habel says, toward

> listening to, and identifying with, Earth as a presence or voice within the [biblical] text. Our task is to take up the cause of Earth and the non-human members of the Earth community by sensing their presence in the text— whether their presence is suppressed, oppressed or celebrated. We seek to move beyond identifying ecological themes in creation theology to identifying with Earth in its ecojustice struggle.[1]

Traditional biblical exegesis had stripped the natural world of its agency, its subjecthood, its voice. A new hermeneutic (or theory of interpretation) of biblical Earth solidarity challenges the personal salvation model of conventional Christianity and its occasional indifference to the wonder and suffering of creation. A new hermeneutic of Earth solidarity is a recovery of the Bible's lost witness to the beauty of creation, as well as its message of prophetic judgment against all of us in the human community who have emptied the natural world of God's presence and then desecrated and despoiled the planet accordingly.

At first glance, an Earth-centered biblical hermeneutic might be misunderstood as tendentiously "constructing" the Bible's meaning rather than objectively "discovering" what the Bible actually says. Are green biblical hermeneutics an exercise in *eisegetically* reading one's own biases and interests "into" the scriptural text rather than *exegetically* reading "out" of the text the true meaning of its authoritative teachings? In response, I think a rigidly framed eisegesis/exegesis distinction trades on a false alternative. There is no "pure" reading of the biblical texts—or, indeed, any collection of texts—that is not shaped by the founding presuppositions of the reader. No reader is a *tabula rasa* that simply passively records a text's inherent message; on the contrary, all reading is an active construal of the text's potential range of meanings based on the reader's animating engagement with these potentialities. These possible lines of meaning are a product of the encounter between the world of the reader and the world of the text, to paraphrase interpretation theorists Hans-Georg Gadamer and Paul Ricoeur.[2] In this model, the hermeneutical task consists of the reader submitting her orienting worldview to the vertiginous and exciting give-and-take between text and reader, reader and text, and is the hallmark of all great works of literature and art.

Since all texts, including the biblical texts, yield a possible range of meanings, not just one timeless message, the question for me is, What is the Bible saying to us today? I encounter the Bible as a living voice of ongoing revelation that speaks afresh to each generation. I freely grant that a green reading of the Bible as an earthen vessel in part is a reflection of the twenty-first-century concern with the tenuous well-being of our planet's delicate ecosystem in an era of unprecedented environmental degradation. But I would also suggest that Sojourner Truth's abolitionist biblical hermeneutic in the nineteenth century, or Martin Luther King, Jr.'s nonviolent reading of the Bible in the twentieth, were also attempts to recover the scriptural texts' ancient wisdom regarding the most crucial issues of their time. Did these previous readers impose their own value systems onto the Bible and force it to speak against the grain of its potentially liberatory lines of meaning? I do not think so. It is this interpretive struggle to engage the Bible on its own terms so that it can speak again to the pressing concerns and passions of our generation that is the focus of Earth-based hermeneutics.

The Green Jesus

One of the best ways to rehabilitate Christianity's earthen identity is through a nature-based retrieval of the person of Jesus as the green face of God in the world. Recovering the Gospel narratives through environmental optics opens up Jesus' ministry as a celebration of the beauty of the Earth and committed search for justice for all the denizens of the good creation God has made. Jesus is a green prophet: he ministered to the poor and forgotten members of society and criticized extreme

wealth based on a disregard of one's neighbor and exploitation of the gifts of creation. In the horrifying story of the
Rich Man and Lazarus in Luke 16, Jesus sketched a contrast
between a rich man, who feasted sumptuously on a daily basis,
and Lazarus, riddled with pus-filled sores and licked by dogs,
whose diet consisted of scraps off the rich man's table. In all of
the Gospels Jesus reserves some of his harshest judgment for
this rich man, who is consigned to a fiery hell and punished
for his wasteful lifestyle and lack of regard for Lazarus. Jesus
regularly speaks truth to power by criticizing the affluent, who
take advantage of nature's bounty and push the poor into lives
of chronic suffering and ill health.

Jesus' ministry of green compassion plunged him into the
heart of human misery, often at a great cost to himself. In
Mark 6 he learns of the public beheading of John the Baptist
by Herod Antipas.[3] Then and now, ritual decapitation is a
particularly grisly form of state-sponsored terrorism. Shattered
by this spectacle, Jesus traveled by boat with his followers to
mourn John's death in a lonely place, only to be greeted by
the area townspeople—five thousand strong, according to the
story. "As he went ashore, he saw a great crowd; and he had
compassion for them, because they were like sheep without
a shepherd" (Mark 6:34). As it was growing late, the local
crowd became hungry, and Jesus asked his followers to feed
the thousands who had gathered to meet him. They did so,
miraculously, by distributing five loaves and two fish to everyone in the assembly.

Jesus knew what lay ahead for him by allying with John
the Baptist and continuing to raise the profile of his public ministry. This feeding miracle further placed him in the
crosshairs of Herod's anger and resentment. In this narrative

he partnered with Earth to bring forth an overabundant meal for the renewal of his listeners. Mourning John's death, and presumably fearful for his life, he turned to the good gifts of creation—bread and fish—for the refreshment and sustenance of the crowds who followed him. Earth's bounty gives of itself for all beings' renewal, so Jesus gave of himself in ministry and healing so that all can be fed, materially and otherwise.

The summer after my junior year in college I journeyed to Hong Kong as a short-term student missionary and, through a lack of oversight and miscommunication, ended up establishing my residence in a brothel. The Kowloon guest house where I lived had been a legitimate operation in its recent past, but in the summer of 1978 it was a boarding house for prostitutes. In my *naïveté* I was not clear at first about the nature of my surroundings, but after a couple of weeks I realized what type of establishment I was in. It was an intimate setting: I shared the same bathrooms and general living quarters with some of my housemates, and one young woman from the Philippines named Rosaria became my friend over time.

Rosaria, a devout Roman Catholic, started as a cocktail waitress in an upscale international hotel restaurant and later became a sex worker in different parts of the city. She sent a portion of her earnings to her family in the hope of returning to the Philippines with enough money to move with her children away from her abusive partner and support her family on her own. My friend was a victim of this man's violent impulses, but she was also a victim of a global economic system that preys on the misfortunes of the dispossessed by converting their assets, in this case Rosaria's sexualized body, into capital. Well-heeled Japanese, American, and European businessmen traveled to Hong Kong to purchase Rosaria for an hour or an afternoon. So, in addition to being beat up by her partner, Rosaria also suffered the violence of becoming a commodity for further use and abuse in the global economy. Growing up in an urban slum, she had no access to education, healthcare, childcare, or workforce development. In desperation, she was willing to trade one form of violence (domestic abuse) for another (the sex trade).

Rosaria became Christ to me during my summer in Hong Kong. I came to the then-British Colony to do missionary work, but instead I was evangelized about the true meaning of the Gospel. Beyond the Bible studies and youth events I coordinated that summer, it was time spent with Rosaria that proved transformative. Like Jesus, she sacrificed her flesh so that her children could live. Shamed and humiliated by the Catch-22 choice she felt compelled to make—stay at home and suffer abuse, or leave her family in the hope of returning someday with adequate resources—Rosaria modeled to me a life of compassion in the face of soul-killing, home-based, and large-scale structural oppression. As best as she knew how, she took up her cross of daily suffering in order to liberate her family from violence and grinding poverty.

Neil Darragh writes beautifully about the "deep incarnation" of Jesus—an enfleshment "into the very tissue of biological existence"—to underscore God's compassionate care for the community of all living things.[4] Like Rosaria, who gave herself for the others she loved, Jesus came into the pain of a broken world to set free the oppressed for a better life. In Rosaria's case, the oppressed were her family in the Philippines. From the perspective of the contemporary import of Jesus' integrated social-environmental ministry, today the oppressed include both the economic cast offs in our global economy, such as Rosaria, and the "new poor," that is, the increasingly degraded and impoverished nonhuman members of Earth community.[5]

Jesus' deep incarnation, his human birth, took place in a marginal environment embedded within the natural world. With no place to stay among the traveling public, he was birthed in a stable and placed in a feeding trough used by farm animals. Jesus entered consciousness already intimate, then, with the plight of the human poor and the rhythms and flow patterns of agricultural life. Environmentally speaking, the expanse of nonhuman nature played a crucial role in his baptism as well: full immersion in the Jordan river prepared Jesus for his work ahead, and God appeared as a bird, the Holy Spirit who hovered over him as he emerged from the Jordan. After his baptism, Jesus inaugurated his public ministry by preaching the good news to the poor, the sick, and the oppressed, and then he departed alone into the desert for forty days. In this vision quest in the wild, he began a life long practice of finding peace and sustenance through regular sojourns into wilderness areas. His first miracle turned water into wine at Cana—a celebration of the goodness of the fruit of earthen vines that hearkened back to his miracle of the bread and fishes—and his first miracle with his inner circle of disciples was a fish catch of overwhelming numbers—another kind of celebration of the goodness of creation. In turn, the last supper was a group meal that anticipated the saving death of Jesus by celebrating the good gifts of creation—eating bread and drinking wine.

Many of Jesus' parables—the lilies of the field, the birds of the air, the lost sheep, the mustard seed, the sower and the seed, and the great banquet—are demonstrations of the natural world as the expression of God's loving and just relations with the world of humans, animals, and plants. Indeed, the food web itself is infused with divine power: "Look at the birds of the air," Jesus says in the Sermon on the Mount, "they neither sow nor reap nor gather into barns, and yet your heavenly Father feeds them" (Matthew 6:26). God feeds our avian kin, Jesus implied, through interlocking food chains. God is not an external force far removed from the concerns of everyday plants and animals, but, animistically, the interanimating power of the life web necessary for the survival and fruition of all beings, human and nonhuman alike. God lives in and through the miracle of photosynthesis—the herbivores that live off plant species, the carnivores like us that eat other plants and animals, and the decomposers that break down dead tissues and thereby reenergize the soil for renewed plant growth. The food web is the sacred matrix, energized by divine compassion, that makes everyday existence possible.

The beauty of life on Earth is a major theme in Jesus' ecological justice ministry. His judgment against the rich who exploit nature's gifts and his vision of God's power in the life-web are grounded in his aesthetic wonder at the splendor of life on Earth. Consider again the Sermon on the Mount: "Consider the lilies of the field, how they grow; they neither toil nor spin; yet I tell you, even Solomon in all of his glory was not clothed like one of these" (Matt. 6:29). Jesus, the everyday botanist, invoked the magic of flowers to illustrate the beauty of existence on this lush, velvet planet. The pleasures of the sensuous life are basic to his ministry. Roadside lilies envelope the viewer in dark purples, rich oranges, and dazzling whites; they surround all passersby aromatherapeutically with heady scents and healing perfumes. Alive with color and fragrance, these tall, showy flowers are often marked with contrasting delicate spots or elegant brushstroke colors. None of the magnificently built structures associated with the historic grandeur of King Solomon's reign—the original Jerusalem Temple that housed the Ark of the Covenant and Ten Commandments, along with elaborate palaces, urban waterworks, and impressive stables and military installations—compares with the fragrant, colorful flowering plants that grace our ordinary existence. The dazzling architectural wonders of Israel's Golden Age were the products of Solomon's hard labor and ingenuity, but Jesus' lilies do nothing to achieve the commonplace elegance that outshines even Solomon's spectacular monuments. Jesus, the green animist, turns upside-down the aesthetic value system we use to judge beauty—washed in the marvel and perfume of wild lilies, he allows us to be reborn as patrons and guardians of the free gifts God offers us in the bounty and wonder of creation. Less is more, says Jesus, and what is free and wild is better than anything we can plan and develop. Jesus' raw, unfiltered joy and pleasure in the blessings of the good, green Earth is the basis of our work toward earthen renewal and the deliverance of our planet home from destruction.[6]

Jesus' major sermons took place at natural sites saturated with divine power—the Mount of Olives, the Garden of Gethsemane, the Pool at Siloam—and his famous self-referential sayings were consistently drawn from nature—"I am the bread of life, I am the true vine, I am the good shepherd." In a phrase, Jesus was an *animist with a social conscience.* He experienced divinity everywhere within nature—he saw and felt God alive in every person, animal, rock, tree, and body of water he encountered. His animism was one of the driving forces behind his radically this-worldly model of political engagement. When pressed about his role as Messiah—a king that would deliver Israel from its enemies—he replied that his new kingdom is not a faraway future reality, but rather is already being realized now in the good creation God has made. "The kingdom of God is not coming with things that can be observed," he said to his critics, "for, the kingdom of God is in fact among you" (Luke 17:20-21). But Jesus' politics of here-and-now transformation got him into trouble. Seeking to spread his already-present kingdom through works of compassion and justice, he was charged with sedition by the Roman state and crucified.

In the Christian story, the cross is green. It is green because Jesus' witness on the cross is to a planet where all of God's children are bearers of life-giving Spirit. It is green because the goodness of creation is God's here-and-now dwelling place where everyday life is charged with sacred presence and power. The kingdom of God is not some far-off possibility never to be realized on Earth; rather, it is the always-here reality of God's enfleshed presence *now* being realized through caring for one's neighbor and seeking justice for the oppressed. By modeling our lives after Jesus' life, we realize the truth of the prophetic teaching, "By his bruises we are healed" (Isaiah 53:5). Jesus' suffering on behalf of all of us who cry out for restoration and compassion, human and nonhuman alike, enables us, in turn, to reach out to a dangerously warming planet and heal it as well. It is in this sense that his suffering makes us whole—his life of service empowers us to commit ourselves to social justice and planetary well-being. We work to blunt the now inexorable impacts of climate change and species loss because Jesus labored and suffered on our behalf in order to bring healing to a broken world. The kingdom of

God is in our midst. In the power of the green cross, our task is to realize the gospel truth that this sacred Earth is God's kingdom where the vital needs of all of God's children are to be met with compassion and integrity.

The Carnal Spirit

Along with a rediscovery of the green Jesus, a second approach to recovering Christianity's earthen identity is through a creation-based study of the Holy Spirit. Thich Nhat Hanh, the Vietnamese Buddhist monk and Christian discussion-partner, writes that when "we touch the Holy Spirit, we touch God not as a concept but as a living reality."[7] A retrieval of the Spirit's disclosure of herself in the biblical literatures as one with the four cardinal elements—earth, air, water, and fire—is one more means by which Christianity's carnal identity can be established—not as a concept, but as a living reality, or better, as a living being.[8] (Incidentally, I will use the female pronoun throughout this book to name the Spirit, based on some compelling scriptural precedence.[9]) As Jesus' ministry was undergirded by his intimate communion with the natural world, so also is the work of the Spirit biblically understood according to the primal elements that constitute biological existence.

As *earth* the Spirit is portrayed or symbolized as an earthen, avian life form—a dove—who is God's helping, nurturing, inspiring, and birthing presence in creation. The mother Spirit Bird in the opening creation song of Genesis, like a giant hen sitting on her cosmic nest egg, broods over the planet and brings all things into life and fruition. In turn, this same hovering Spirit Bird, as a dove that alights on Jesus as he comes up through the waters of his baptism, appears in all four of the

Gospels to signal God's approval of Jesus' public work. This winged, feathered God actualizes an Earth-based communion in which all beings are filled with divine presence, heaven and earth are unified, and God and nature are one (Genesis 1:1-2; Matthew 3:13-17, Mark 1:9-11; Luke 3:21-22; John 1:29-34).

As *air* the Spirit is both the animating divine breath who brings into existence all living things (Genesis 2:7; Psalms 104:29-30) and the wind of prophecy and judgment who renews and transforms those she possesses and indwells (Judges 6:34; John 3:6-8; Acts 2:1-4). *Rûach* (Hebrew) and *pneuma* (Greek) are the biblical terms for Spirit; they mean breath, air, or wind. The breathy God is closer to us than we are to ourselves. In meditation when we say, "Focus on your breath," in essence we are saying, "Focus on God." Our lives are framed, and made possible, by the always-there gift of divine wind. We enter consciousness drawing our first breath—we inhale God at the moment of our birth. And we exhale God with our last breath—we pass into death by evacuating the aerial Spirit from our mortal bodies. The Holy Spirit is God's invigorating, life-giving presence within the atmosphere who sustains our need-for-air existence and the existence of all creatures on the planet.

As *water* the Spirit brings life and healing to all who are baptized and drink from her eternal springs (John 3:1-15, 4:1-30, 7:37-38; Acts 8:26-40, 11:1-18). True thirst, true desire, and true need is satiated by drinking the liquid Spirit who soaks God's followers with a deep sense of wholeness and joy. In the eucharist, we eat God in the bread and drink God in the wine. In this act we are reminded that all of Earth's vital fluids that make planetary existence possible—blood, mucus, tears, milk, semen, sweat, urine—are infused with sacred energy.

Again, as with earth and air, life is a primordial gift in which God graces all things with the necessary elements for survival and full fruition. The Water God entertains us with torrential rains, seeping mudholes, rushing rivers, and cascading waterfalls so that life on this juicy, liquid planet can be hydrated and refreshed.

As *fire* the Spirit is the blaze of God that prophetically condemns the wealthy and unjust who exploit others, and the divine spark that ignites the multilingual and multicultural mission of the early church (Matthew 3:11-12; Acts 2:1-4). On the one hand, fire is a harsh metaphor for God's judgment against human arrogance and overly inflated sense of self. But on the other, it is an expression of God's unifying presence in the fledgling church, as happened at Pentecost with the Spirit's incandescent announcement of herself in tongues of fire to a diverse collection of disciples, according to the Book of Acts. This sacred fire erased false differences and consumed the ethnic and cultural divisions that marked the early Christians apart from one another. In the wider biosphere, the Fire God continues as a unifying, vivifying power necessary for the well-being of planetary life: fire cooks our food, heats our homes, powers our transportation systems, and maintains our planet's temperate climate. Without the gift of fire we would all perish, but with our dumping of carbon into the atmosphere, we have unleashed the sun's lethal potential and perverted nature's balance by producing a superheated weather system that will endanger the survival of future generations.

To be human is to live in spiritual harmony with the primary elements. A full life consists of everyday gratitude and care for the elemental gifts of natural existence. In part, this elemental sensibility is recoverable by a return to historic belief and practice. Ancient Christian belief teaches that God is present to us "under the elements" of bread and wine. Putting the carnal Spirit model to work, this belief is deemed ever so true and now expanded as well: beyond bread and wind, God's Spirit continues to be real under *all* of the cardinal elements—earth, air, water, fire—that constitute the building blocks of life. While the Holy Spirit (or the "Holy Ghost") is sometimes regarded as a vague and disembodied phantom irrelevant to religious belief or planetary existence, the Bible tells a different story of a radically embodied God who incarnates Godself as Spirit in the four elements. Correspondingly, and using language borrowed from French philosopher Luce Irigaray, Ellen Armour develops an "elemental theology" in which God is known and loved through the primal elements. By reimagining core liturgical practices in accord with the elemental dynamics of bodily existence, Armour injects new life—new *elemental* life—into the ritual heart of Christian faith:

> The central Christian rituals, baptism and eucharist, connect immediately with water and earth. The waters of baptism signify the move from sin to redemption, death to rebirth. The grain and grapes that become bread and wine (and ultimately body and blood) are products of earth and water. The Feast of Pentecost celebrates the descent of the Holy Spirit—in the form of "divided tongues, as of fire" (Acts 2:3)—on Christ's apostles, endowing their ministry with new authority as each listener heard the gospel message in his or her own native tongue. The Feast of the Ascension calls attention to air as the medium through

which Christ ascends, thus linking the heavens and the
Earth, human and the divine. . . . We are quite literally
sustained by air, water, and earth—physically and, if we
adopt this way of thinking, spiritually. We have, then, religious and moral obligations to the natural world. Elemental theology repositions the relationship between divinity,
humanity and the natural world. . . . The elements bind
all three together in a fragile network of interdependency
rather than domination.[10]

Let's look more closely at one of the elemental metaphors
of the Spirit in Christian tradition, namely, the manifestation
of the third member of the Trinity as an avian life-form—the
bird God, as it were, of the biblical witness. In the story of
Jesus' baptism in the four gospels, the Spirit Bird, an earthen
life-form, came down from heaven as a dove—"and the Holy
Spirit descended upon him in *bodily form [Gk. somatikos], as
a dove*" (Luke 3:22)—and lovingly alighted on Jesus' person,
perching protectively on his head and shoulders, as God's
voice of parental love and pride is heard by all present, saying, "This is my beloved Son, with whom I am well pleased."
In the miracle of the incarnation Christians believe that God
literally became *human flesh* in the person of Jesus. But note
here that God also literally became *animal flesh* in the sacred
dove witnessed to in Jesus' baptism. The clear force of the
Greek adverb *somatikos* (literally, to be "bodily" or "corpo-
really") that describes the Spirit's avian arrival in this scene
denotes the embodiment of the Spirit in animal flesh. God, in
sum, is a physical creature, a living thing, an animal on the
order of the birds, fish, and land fauna that inhabit Earth.

Hope for Change

To be sure, the scandal of Christian faith has always been rooted in the belief in the enfleshment of divinity in mortal form. But this scandal must be deepened by reestablishing divine enfleshment not just with reference to Jesus (as human), but with reference to the Spirit (as nonhuman animal). The New Testament's doctrine of incarnation is one of the great teachings of Christian faith. But the true, and generally forgotten, meaning of "incarnation"—from the Latin *carnus*, which means "flesh" or "meat"—is that God incarnated Godself *both* in Jesus *and* Spirit—both as human and nonhuman animal life-forms. The full implications of this realization can only be imagined as Christianity broadens the circle of God's identity and compassion to include not only the human sphere but also the wider expanse of nonhuman living beings. In becoming all things—human and nonhuman—the biblical witness testifies to us that God eagerly desires the health and vitality of the whole created order, not just the human sphere.

In addition to the incarnation, where Jesus and Spirit are united as carnal expressions of God, Jesus and Spirit are further united in suffering and death. Here I have said that the Spirit is a carnal being biblically figured according to the four basic elements—earth, air, water, fire—that constitute our planetary existence. God's gift of Godself to creation is the interanimating Spirit who ensouls all living things with her sustaining force and life-giving power. Nature's elements are not mere symbols or tokens of the Spirit's earthly presence; they are the life-ways that Spirit animates to ensure planetary balance. Correspondingly, when the primary elements are degraded and the overall integrity of creation is threatened, the Spirit, God's generative reality in the biosphere, suffers loss and injury as well. The gift of Spirit in creation is a clue, then, to the Spirit's Earth-based, *cruciform* suffering in our time. The Spirit, the God of flesh and feathers who is one with the natural world, suffers loss and deprivation just like Jesus, but now not the loss of the cross but the loss of Earth community as it bears the corrosive impact of environmental depredation. While Jesus suffered on the cross for the sins of the world, the Spirit in the Earth suffers for the degradation of the world. Jesus suffered because he bore the sins of the world in his human flesh, while the Spirit endures the pain of a degraded Earth in her unity with creation.

The crucified Jesus and the cruciform Spirit are bound together in common affliction. The cut marks of human sin written onto the body of the crucified God in Jesus' passion are now re-written across the expanse of the whole planet as the wounded Spirit bears the incisions of her own passion, the passion of planetary abuse. Jesus' agony and the distress of the Spirit are one. Our unsustainable lifestyles that damage Earth community—the impact of global warming on extreme weather events, ocean acidification, biodiversity loss, and desertification—result in deep injury to God's Spirit. The Spirit, then, as the green face of God in the world, has become in our time as Jesus was in his time, the wounded body of God. Whenever forms of life that swim and fly and crawl and run upon the Earth are wantonly threatened and destroyed, the Spirit experiences death and trauma in herself. Whenever our greed and ambition strips creation of its beauty and its bounty, the Spirit is exploited and abused. Whenever Earth community is laid to waste, the Spirit deeply mourns this loss and fragmentation.

Nevertheless, just as Jesus' suffering offered redemption and hope, so also does the suffering of Spirit in Earth community promise God's abiding presence within all things. In Jesus' wounds we are healed. We saw above, because his suffering for us models how to care for others. Similarly, the Spirit's suffering teaches us how to pray and act and thereby empowers us to live on behalf of the biosphere as creation groans under the onslaughts to ecological well-being for all of God's creatures. In Jesus' wounds we are renewed, and in the Spirit's wounds we are healed as well. As in Paul's time, creation continues to be bound and fettered by humankind's refusal to live within proper limits. All of creation, Paul wrote, is groaning under the weight of human sin; in our time, human *ecological* sin is crushing the Earth as we destroy vital ecosystems necessary for our and others' survival. Said Paul:

> The creation itself will be set free from its bondage to decay and obtain the freedom of the glory of the children of God. We know that the whole creation has been groaning in labor pains until now; and not only the creation, but we ourselves, who have the first fruits of the Spirit, groan inwardly as we wait for adoption, the redemption of our bodies. (Romans 8:21-23)

Creation is in bondage to ruin and decay, Paul said, but now we see daily *how* it is spiraling toward certain destruction, at least for human habitation, if we cannot reverse our abusive lifestyles and practice everyday sustainability. But through our prayers and sighs and tears inspired by the Spirit's presence— as we, and all beings, groan and yearn in our depths for redemption—our wills are empowered to make the changes necessary for a green future.

Here I have sought to make the case that Jesus' and the Spirit's ecological identities are reawakened through a recovery of the New Testament's ancient wisdom that God is radically enfleshed within all things. This move to encountering the deep interdependence between God and creation—this move to Christian animism—is a necessary step in harnessing the potential of Christian faith to address the current Earth crisis. Apart from a deep green reawakening of Christianity's central teaching—namely, that all creation is literally Spirit-filled as embodied in the life and message of Jesus—it will be impossible for many persons to experience a spiritually charged connection to the land that is our common home and common destiny. With this deep connection as foundational to Earth-based spirituality, the potential is realized for engaged citizenship to combat the crises of global warming and species loss in our dangerous era, and the prospects of saving our planet, and thereby saving ourselves, are heightened indeed.

Chapter Three

ENJOY THE FLESH

"You gave me no kiss, but from the time I came in she has not stopped kissing my feet." (Luke 7:45)

Erotic Hospitality

In the previous chapter I portrayed Jesus as the green prophet who saw God in all things and the Spirit as the God of flesh and feathers who presents herself according to the four primary elements. My goal was to tap into the green roots of Christian faith in order to nurture a spiritually charged commitment to saving our common habitat, Earth. This earthen theology now paves the way for a deeper understanding of the core Christian affirmation of the goodness and the delights of the body as well. If God enfleshed Godself in Jesus, and the Spirit manifests Godself in earth, air, water, and fire, then all things bodily and fleshy are good—and the many wonderful pleasures of the body, including sexual pleasure, are good as well. Christian theology has often missed this point, however. Paul, for example, wrote that "It is well for a man not to touch a woman" (1 Cor. 7:1), rendering ancient Christianity anxious and troubled about the role of the body and sexual expression in spiritual life.

Nevertheless, many Christians today have moved into a joyous space where sexual intimacy and pleasure are valued as primary sites of God's presence in human community.[1] This emergence into what I would call "carnal spirituality" is nourished by the endearing scriptural narratives of sexual and nonsexual touching that challenge the soul-deadening disregard for bodily pleasure in some of the central teachings of ancient Christianity. The biblical celebration of erotic pleasure reaches a crescendo in the Song of Solomon ("O may your breasts be like clusters of the vine, and the scent of your breath like apples, and your kisses like the best wine," 7:8-9) and continues with stories about Jesus' scandalously fleshly, transgressive acts of sexually nuanced touching and being touched. By way of celebrating the body-affirming potential of biblical Christianity, the exegesis of one of these ancient stories in the New Testament around the theme of erotic hospitality is the focal point of this chapter.

After a brief introduction to early Christian attitudes toward bodily desire, my focus falls on the "sinful woman"—or better, the "woman who loved too much"—in Luke 7:36-50, who lovingly massages, wets, and kisses Jesus' feet, perhaps preparing them for his burial. This unnamed woman wets Jesus' feet with her tears, rubs them with her hair, kisses them with her mouth, and anoints them with a sweet-smelling lotion. Noting the importance of this story for biblical erotics, I focus on how

Jesus embraces the scandal that this robustly sensual encounter generates ("from the time I came in she has not stopped kissing my feet," 7:45) in order to articulate his message of "welcoming the body" as central to his mission.

Next, I compare this Lukan story of deep touching with the healing intimacies between Ruth and Boaz, a widowed Gentile and her Hebrew kinsman in the Book of Ruth; and Sethe and Paul D, two former slaves in Toni Morrison's novel, *Beloved*. While the ancient practice of arranged marriage, along with the modern slave trade, generally trafficked in flesh as a market commodity, Ruth and Boaz, on the one hand, and Sethe and Paul D, on the other, develop, against the greatest of odds, their own rituals of erotic play and healing. The enfleshed sensuality of biblical and Morrisonian touching celebrates, welcomes, and heals flesh as sacred gift. Through the Lukan woman's and Jesus' passion for intimacy, and echoing the Book of Ruth and *Beloved*, I conclude with the outlines of a biblically inflected "haptology " (Gk., *haptos*)—a theology of touching—with the potential to heal our culture of its abuse of one another's flesh and to teach us to love our own and others' innermost desires for pleasure, intimacy, friendship, and love.

War against the Flesh

Much of early Christianity is a sustained polemic against bodily instincts, sexual desire, and even the institution of marriage itself. The three biblical sources for these arguments are (1) Jesus' valorization of voluntary, self-imposed celibacy in Matthew 19:12 ("For there are eunuchs who have been have been made eunuchs by others, and there are eunuchs who have made themselves eunuchs for the sake of the kingdom of heaven. Let anyone accept this who can"); (2) Jesus' proposal in Matthew 22:30 that married couples, postmortem, will be angel-like, single people again ("For in the resurrection [spouses] they neither marry nor are given in marriage, but are like angels in heaven"); and (3) Paul's ascetic ideal in 1 Corinthians 7:8-9 that marriage, while not a model state for Christians, is sometimes necessary as a prophylactic to fend off uncontrollable lust ("To the unmarried and the widows I say that it is well for them to remain unmarried as I am. But if they are not practicing self-control, they should marry. For it is better to marry than to be aflame with passion").

Privileging celibacy allowed early Christians to position themselves as religiously superior to their "fleshly" cousins in the Jewish world of the first and second centuries CE. As a celibate who put under control his sexual desires, Paul distinguished between the Gentile Christian "children of promise," who are the true heirs of God's covenant with Israel, and the Jewish "children of the flesh," whose covenant with God, while not abrogated, is now expanded to include Jewish and non-Jewish followers of Jesus (Rom 9:1-13). Paul and his patristic successors became masters of allegorical biblical hermeneutics in which the "living spirit" of the Christian gospel supersedes the "dead letter" of Jewish law. Sexual renunciation and spiritual circumcision became tangible signs of this new figurative reading of the Torah and the commandments. In the writings of Paul and other early church leaders, the old observance of the law relied on outward, physical signs of obedience to Torah (especially having children and being circumcised), whereas the new fidelity to Christ takes leave of the body in favor of the inner faith of the believer. While procreation and circumcision were basic to Jewish observance based on the Genesis commands to "be fruitful and multi-ply" (1:22) and "Every male among you shall be circumcised" (17:10), these corporeal covenants were spiritualized and set aside by Paul in favor of his proposal that "he who marries his fianceé does well; and he who refrains from marriage will do better" (1 Cor. 7:38), and his notion that "true circumcision" is not "external and physical" but "a matter of the heart—it is spiritual and not literal" (Rom. 2:28-29). True covenantal life with God is a spiritual exercise of the heart, not a product or a mark of the flesh. Inward fidelity to Jesus and the gospel now supplants outward duty to Torah.

Paul's move away from the outward activities of procreative sex and circumcision to the inner life of the Spirit marked a distinct step in the evolution of early Christianity from its Jewish origins.[2] The physical reality of Israel and the sexualized, circumcised Jewish body were now supplanted by the "new Israel" of the church and the holy Christian body, which has taken leave of the flesh (read: sexuality, procreation, and circumcision) in order to realize the ideal of pure, sexless, unmarried life in the Spirit. Virginal purity was now the insignia of genuine Christianity—a cultural oddity in antiquity that opened up an unbridgeable rift, as Daniel Boyarin writes, between early Christianity and formative Judaism:

> In spite of the enormous variations within both Christianities and rabbinic Judaism, the near-universal privileging of virginity, even for Christian thinkers who valorize marriage, produces an irreducible difference between that [Christian] formation and rabbinic Judaism, for which sexuality and procreation are understood as acts of ultimate religious significance and for which virginity is

highly problematic, as Christian writers in antiquity correctly emphasized.[3]

Over and against formative Judaism, the New Testament's deprecation of the body and sexual desire rendered many subsequent early Christian leaders "athletes of God," in historian of antiquity Peter Brown's phrase, who made war against their flesh in order to cultivate their spiritual natures.[4] Origen, the third-century Christian allegorical theologian, literally interpreted Jesus' blessing regarding those who "made themselves eunuchs for the sake of the kingdom of heaven" (Matt. 19:12) and at age twenty castrated himself. As a virgin for Christ no longer dominated by his sexual and physical drives, Origen graphically appropriated Jesus' counsel about celibacy and became a perfect vessel for the display of the Spirit.[5] Origen's celibate athleticism is further underscored by the extracanonical fifth-century text, Pseudo-Titus, which offers a sustained exhortation to celibacy and monastic rigor as a badge of purity and holiness.[6] The author calls on young men to be like the mythological phoenix, a paradigm of virginal solitude, who achieved holiness by avoiding female temptation:

> Above all the ascetic should avoid women on that account and see to it that he does (worthily) the duty entrusted to him by God. . . . O man, who understands nothing at all of the fruits of righteousness, why has the Lord made the divine phoenix and not given it a little wife, but allowed it to remain in loneliness? Manifestly only on purpose to show the standing of virginity, i.e., that young men, remote from intercourse with women, should remain holy.[7]

In the Christian West, Augustine appeared most responsible for early Christian antagonism toward sex and the body. Extending Paul's dictum that "For what the flesh desires is opposed to the spirit, and what the spirit desires is opposed to the flesh" (Gal. 5:17), Augustine maintained that human beings are ruled by carnal desire (*concupiscence)* as a result of Adam's fall from grace in the garden of Eden. All people are now "in Adam," as it were, since Adam's sin is transferred to his offspring—the human race—through semen, what Augustine called the "seminal substance from which we were to be propagated."[8] As historian of early Christianity Elaine Pagels puts it, "That semen itself, Augustine argues, already 'shackled by the bond of death,' transmits the damage incurred by sin. Hence, Augustine concludes, every human being ever conceived through semen already is born contaminated with sin."[9] In their fleshly bodies, seminally generated infants are tainted with "original sin" communicated to them through their biological parents' sexual intercourse. To put this point bluntly, the fetus is damned at the moment of conception—even before birth—because it is contaminated by Adam's primordial transgression through the transmission of semen during the conjugal act. Augustine further asserted that physical weakness, bodily suffering, and sexual desire (*libido*) itself are signs that the corporal, material world is under God's judgment. "Ever since Eden, however, spontaneous sexual desire is, Augustine contends, the clearest evidence of the effect of original sin."[10] Thus, without the infusion of supernatural grace, all of creation—as depraved and corrupted—is no longer amenable to the influence of God's love and power. Augustine's division between spirit and sex, religion and desire, and God and the body was an ugly splitting that survives in our own time—an era, often in the name of religion, marked by deep anxiety about and hostility toward human sexuality, the body, and the natural world in general.

Along with Jesus' elevation of celibacy, Paul's proscriptions against marriage and Augustine's linkage between original sin and erotic desire continue to cast a long shadow over the churches' teachings about sexuality. Many scholars today regard Paul's and Augustine's sexual theologies as bedrock to contemporary Christians' negative attitudes toward sex and the body:

> Paul and Augustine are two theologians who stand at the headwaters of the Christian religion. They have bequeathed to Christianity an anti-sexual legacy that lingers to this day. Or to express the matter colloquially, traditional Christianity had deliberately chosen to take a dim view of sex. Take, by way of example, the church's veneration of celibacy (the state of having no sex by having no spouse). With its commitment to the concept of the divided self and with its veneration of Saint Paul, who wished that all people were unmarried like him (1 Cor 7:7), the church over the centuries has applauded celibacy. Prior to Christianity's emergence, perpetual celibacy was practiced in neither the Gentile nor Jewish worlds (an exception was the Essene community at Qumran). To be unmarried and childless was—especially for Jews—a disgrace. But Christianity introduced a new way of viewing perpetual celibacy.[11]

It is against the backdrop of this sort of sexless spirituality in early Christianity—an ideal that divided Christianity from Judaism in antiquity—that I will sketch the erotic hospitality of the Lukan Jesus. Alongside the early church's "majority report" concerning noncorporeal Christian existence, I analyze Luke's "minority report" of Jesus' and the anonymous woman's transgressive and erotically charged interactions as a counterpoint to the mainstream ideal.

The Unnamed Woman and Erotic Care of Bodies

The sexual body is a privileged site of divine encounter in the Lukan story of the unnamed woman who washes Jesus' feet. At Simon the Pharisee's dinner party, an anonymous woman enters Simon's home and lovingly wets Jesus' feet with her tears and hair. Uninvited, she approaches Jesus from behind, lets down her hair and begins to wash and anoint his feet with a jar of perfume, her hair, and her many tears. Throughout this initial encounter, significantly, Jesus does not speak. Simon wonders to himself how Jesus, claiming to be a prophet, could allow this sort of woman, perhaps a prostitute, to touch him. As if reading Simon's thoughts, Jesus tells a parable about two debtors and how the one who owes the most, once forgiven his debts, now loves the most. Simon understands the meaning of the parable; and Jesus, in one of his classic man-bites-dog reversals of the social order, publicly rebukes Simon for not fully welcoming him to his home and then praises the kissing woman for her "great love" (Luke 7:47). Like many of Jesus' narratives, the story inverts established expectations. Who is the real sinner, the true lover, the authentic follower of Jesus in this account: Simon, the established religious leader, or the notoriously sinful woman? At the end, Jesus forgives the woman of her sins and offers her God's peace, which provokes much questioning and likely criticism among Simon's dinner guests.

As with many biblical narratives, the scandal and irony of this story are lost to many of us today. Like other scriptural texts, this story has been domesticated by some commentators' appeal to the putative "religious" message of divine forgiveness at the story's end and a general disregard of the shock and discomfort the story was intended to generate among its hearers and readers.[12] Using a feminist hermeneutic, I argue that the story is an exercise in erotic performance art that intends to liberate readers into a new relationship with Christ that is body- and pleasure-affirming. I use feminist approaches to examine how Luke 7:36-50 functions as a model of female agency that subversively challenges certain structures of oppression in antiquity. From this perspective, the text can be read as valorizing a particular transgressive practice (the unnamed woman's sexualized foot washing) in order to realize emancipatory possibilities for identity formation against the social and religious distortions of its time.[13]

To begin to make this case, let me offer here a retelling of the story in contemporary terms in order to imagine how the story might speak afresh to the present-day reader.

A Disturbing Incident at Local Minister's Home

Something astonishing took place last week in the home of the Reverend and Mrs. J. Josiah Alexander IV of First Presbyterian Church of Smithtown. As is their custom, the Alexanders invited this year's theologian-in-residence, the Reverend Ian Cameron, to a formal lunch after the morning worship service. A local unemployed woman, reportedly charged this past summer with solicitation, gained access to the house and approached Rev. Cameron just as the Alexanders and guests were sitting down

for supper. Appearing emotionally unstable and crying pro-
fusely, the woman (her name was not disclosed) unloosened
her long hair and proceeded to take off Rev. Cameron's socks
and shoes. She then wet his feet with her tears, rubbed them
with her hair, and kissed them incessantly, or so it appeared.
The woman was wearing a vial of perfume, or similar sub-
stance, around her neck which she also used in her attentions
to Rev. Cameron's feet. To everyone's dismay, Rev. Cameron
allowed these theatrics to continue for quite awhile, and then,
shockingly, rebuked Rev. Alexander (and presumably Mrs.
Alexander) for not properly welcoming him to their home, and
contrasting them unfavorably to this overly wrought woman.

"I entered your home," he said, "and you did not shake my
hand or offer me a hug or kiss, whereas this woman placed my
tired feet in her own hands and has not ceased to kiss me since
I sat down. You did not take my coat, but she took my socks
and shoes and thoughtfully put them aside for me. You did not
offer me a drink, but she continues to massage my feet, refresh-
ing my body and spirit and welcoming me to your home in the
way you should have done. See this woman? She loves me, but
what about you?"

Understandably, the Alexanders and guests were stunned
into silence by Rev. Cameron's reprimand, not expecting a
respected member of the clergy to sanction the behavior of
this uninvited intruder. Equally shocking, Rev. Cameron con-
cluded the woman's visit by telling her that God had forgiven
her sins—a rather remarkable claim for a woman who has
a reputation as a person of ill repute. The event has gener-
ated considerable controversy in Smithtown, where members
of the Mayflower-descended and Princeton-educated Alexan-
der family have been respected pillars of the community for

generations. Younger residents are referring to the scene at the
Alexander home as a "happening," while Rev. Alexander and
elders at First Presbyterian are considering initiating a formal
ecclesiastical review of Rev. Cameron's behavior during the
incident.

With this contemporary retelling as a backdrop, I read the
Lukan story as a countertestimony to mainstream Christian
anxiety about the body and sexuality. In this vein, I see two
crucial issues emerging in an exegesis of its range of meanings: the question of the woman's identity as an urban sinner,
and the quality of her amorous encounter with Jesus as the
basis of God's forgiveness and peace in her life.

Who is the Anonymous Woman?

Much has been written about the phrase in verse 37 that the
unnamed woman in "the city, who was a sinner," when she
learned about Jesus' presence in Simon the Pharisee's house
and came to minister to him. It is possible, but by no means
certain, that the woman was a prostitute. Elizabeth Schüssler
Fiorenza writes that the appellation "sinner" was reserved
in antiquity for criminals or those persons who worked in
disreputable jobs such as tax collectors, servants, domestics,
swineherders, tanners, prostitutes, and so on. Many of these
professions were not available to women (though certain
service jobs and prostitution were options for women). As
well, female prostitutes, as has been the case historically,
lived in brothels in urban areas in the first century. Circum-
stantially, it is possible that this "woman in the city, who was
a sinner" was a prostitute, but to make this claim with any
certitude is a mistake.[14]

While this woman in Luke may or may not have been a prostitute, it is a mistake to identify her with Mary Magdalene who, erroneously, was often read as a prostitute herself in the exegetical history of this narrative. The story of how Mary Magdalene—a steadfast follower of Jesus who bankrolled his early preaching tours (Luke 8:1-3) and was the first eyewitness to the resurrection (John 20:11-18)—became a prostitute has been carefully analyzed by Gail Corrington Streete and others.[15] In part, the conflation of the anonymous woman in Luke and Mary of Magdala—the "harlot-saint" of early Christian mythology—likely stems from the confusing number of Marys within the New Testament (e.g., Mary the mother of Jesus, Mary of Magdalene, and Mary of Bethany, to name just three of the most prominent) that led to a composite "Marian" picture.[16]

Confusion about the woman's identity in the Lukan story is further overdetermined by another layer of misunderstanding in the reception history of this text—namely, the harmonizing of this account with the similar story of the woman who anoints Jesus' head at Bethany in the other gospels. At first glance, Luke 7:36-50 bears a number of formal similarities with Matthew 26:6-13, Mark 14:3-9, and John 12:1-8. Some commentators think that a "single gospel memory" animates each account, but it is especially clear in Luke's narrative that a different message is being advanced.[17] On the one hand, in all four accounts, a woman appears with Jesus in a home environment and uses a costly jar of ointment on his body, perhaps in a gesture of anointment. In each case this act provokes a negative reaction by onlookers, which is complemented by Jesus' defense of the woman. In many regards, however, the differences between the four narratives are more striking than the similarities. Matthew and Mark locate the woman in the house of Simon the leper, while John locates her in the house of Mary, Martha, and Lazarus. Luke puts the woman in the home of Simon the Pharisee. In the non-Lukan accounts, the disciples complain that the ointment should not have been used on Jesus but sold, with the proceeds given to the poor. As well, the Matthean and Markan accounts place the anointing on Jesus' head, not his feet, explicitly associating the anointing with preparing Jesus' body for burial (as does John). On the other hand, however, all three of these versions make no mention of what is central to the story's scandal in Luke's version: the woman's excessive love of Jesus symbolized by her tears and kissing of his feet, and Jesus' forgiveness of the woman's sins.

Erotic Desire between Jesus and the Woman

What is refreshingly distinctive about Luke's story is how its sexually nuanced details foreground the loved and nurtured body as central to Jesus' message of healing and forgiveness. Jesus and the woman engage one another's flesh in tenderness and affection. It is precisely because they perform this, as it were, erotic theatre of the senses that God's power is realized—namely, the woman's sins are forgiven. Note that the relationship between the woman and Jesus is one of mutuality and reciprocity. She approaches him and reaches for his feet, and he welcomes her touch, her tears, her kisses. The Son of God enjoys being fondled by this woman and, in turn, he offers her God's forgiveness and peace. God's hospitality is actualized by the woman's deep welcoming of Jesus' needy body. As Ann Elvey puts it, "the mutual exchange of hospitality between Jesus and the woman is characteristic of the divine visitation."[18]

The power of God's love made manifest in this excessive display of affection is made clear in Simon's initial dismay with Jesus' enjoyment of the woman's stroking of his body. "If this man were a prophet," he says to himself, "he would know what sort of woman is touching him." Simon's assumption is that a true prophet would not allow such a boundary transgression by a woman of such bad reputation. Of course, Luke provocatively reverses Simon's logic, a point no reader could miss: it is precisely *because* this woman is engaging in publicly forbidden behavior and Jesus knows exactly who she is that his identity as a prophet is confirmed. Jesus' divine prophethood is established on the basis of what society regards as sexually polluting behavior, which Jesus now shows to be a privileged site of divine presence and power. At a meal with a Pharisee, where women were likely not welcomed, and in a first-century culture where women were viewed as property or worse, the woman shreds the social order with her bold physicality.

> The woman comes into the midst of a dinner reserved for men, carries a bottle of perfume, unlooses her hair (a particularly erotic action for Jewish perceptions), repeatedly kisses Jesus' feet, and finally in the presence of all the guests does something that belongs in the realm of intimate behavior or even of perverse practices: she anoints his feet.[19]

The woman enters a male space with brio and courage, presumably unfastens and lets down her hair, which is long enough to be used as a makeshift towel, and commences a prolonged wiping, kissing, and anointing of Jesus' feet.

Consider the parallelism between her actions in verse 38 and Jesus' endorsement of the same in verses 44-46. Luke writes that the woman wet Jesus' feet with her tears, wiped them with her hair, kissed them, and anointed them with perfume (7:38). Jesus then replies to Simon that she has wet his feet with her tears, wiped them with her hair, kissed them (continually, he adds), and anointed his feet with perfume (7:44-46). The four Greek verbs employed to describe these actions (*brecho*, to wet; *ekmasso*, to wipe; *kataphileo*, to kiss; *aleipho*, to anoint) and the actions themselves as recounted by Jesus are the same. The parallelism drives home the text's central theme: Jesus' and the woman's amorous performance art signals that excessive desire for the well-being of another's flesh is the grounds for salvation and forgiveness in God's new order of being. "The kingdom of God is among you," says Jesus in Luke 17:21. God's new order is not "out there" waiting to arrive; it is "here and now," as modeled in this parable of love and intimacy.

Commentators on Luke are often uncomfortable with the unabashed sensuality in the passage. Far from the text's being an exercise in biblical *ars erotica*, traditional readers hyped the "sinful" adjective for the woman, assumed she was a prostitute, interpreted her weeping as repentance, and basically saw her as immodest and shameful. As Teresa Hornsby writes, the woman in Luke 7 was not read as a strong, independent agent of her own spiritual and carnal desires for Jesus, but as a sexually suspect, immoral penitent whom Jesus deigns to forgive.

The image of a woman being so lavishly physical with no apparent fear of reprisal and without any shame associated with her act made me glad . . . because I could finally identify with a character in the biblical text, a character who in my initial reading acts independently in blending together the movements of her body with an expression for raw emotion. . . . But when I looked at the interpretation of Luke's passage, I could not find the woman I had read. I was disappointed to discover that this figure has been used since the earliest interpretations as a symbol of every woman's lewdness, as a symbol of a woman's physicality that stands over and against what is "good" and "proper." With very few exceptions, especially in any work prior to the mid-1980s, scholars either call her a prostitute or they claim that the label the narrator gives her of "sinner" (*hamartolos*) surely indicates that the anointing woman is a carnal transgressor; her effusive weeping, they write, must be indicative of sexual, shame-inspired remorse and repentance; her ointment must have come from her prostitute's tool-box; and the fact that she is kissing a strange man can only mean that she is sexually immoral.[20]

Hornsby is correct: in the history of mainstream biblical theology, the woman is not a model of bold love but an object lesson of immorality. Earlier English translations of the Bible use various deprecating subtitles to define the text in this way: The New American Bible titles Luke 7:36-50 "The Pardon of a Sinful Woman," while the Revised Standard Version calls it "A Sinful Woman Forgiven."[21] These subtitles miss the point of the pericope. The story is not about the woman's sinfulness but about her great love for Jesus; it is not about how bad she was, or how promiscuous she now supposedly is, but about how her lavish care of Jesus' flesh overflows "proper" boundaries and realizes God's love; it is not about shameful sexual transgression but about Jesus' and the woman's shameless license to pleasure and heal the body. The passage, then, would be better subtitled as "The Woman Who Loved Too Much," "The Woman Who Could Not Stop Kissing the Lord," or "The Woman Who Loved Jesus with Complete Abandon."[22] In her lavishly erotic relationship with Jesus, the unnamed woman pushes the boundaries of social convention by massaging Jesus' feet with her hair and bodily fluids, leading to her forgiveness and opening to readers then and today new possibilities for sexually charged spiritual and bodily relations.

Jesus' and Boaz's Feet

A cursory reading of the Lukan focus on Jesus' feet reminds readers today, as it has throughout Christian history, of the story of Ruth and Boaz. The Book of Ruth is a post-exilic Hebrew love story that celebrates the inclusion of outsiders within the changing demography of Israel in the third or fourth century B.C.E. Ruth, a Moabite, lives with her mother-in-law, Naomi, outside of Israel when both Ruth's husband and Naomi's husband die. In mourning, Ruth and Naomi decide to relocate to Bethlehem, Naomi's family home, where Ruth meets a member of her extended family, on older man named Boaz. Naomi tells Ruth to wash and perfume herself and after Boaz has had a meal to go and lie down, unannounced, in Boaz's bed, at his feet. "So [Ruth] went down to the threshing floor and did just as her mother-in-law had instructed her. When Boaz had eaten and drunk, and his heart was in a contented mood, he went to lie down at the end of the heap of grain. Then she came stealthily and uncovered his feet, and lay down" (Ruth 3:6-7). Ruth climbs into bed with Boaz, "uncovers his feet" [that is, his genitals] and when he awakens at midnight, she asks him to "spread your skirt over your servant [that is, have sexual relations with her], for you are next of kin" (Ruth 3:9). Boaz agrees and says he will marry her; but to avoid embarrassment, Ruth leaves his bed early the next morning before anyone learns of their encounter the night before. Boaz soon thereafter marries Ruth, and they subsequently have a son name Obed.

Traditional commentaries regard the message of the story to be that Ruth, a non-Jewish foreigner, preserved the family line through which King David emerged by marrying a Hebrew man, Boaz: "The women of the neighborhood named [Ruth's son] Obed, he became the father of Jesse, the father of David" (Ruth 4:17).[23] On this telling, the importance of Ruth is essentially patriarchal and political: she is a place-holder in the Davidic line that preserves the traditional monarchy. In this vein, she is the legal property of whoever becomes her husband. Boaz makes this point clear to Ruth's nearest kinsman regarding the twin purchase of a field owned by Naomi and the person of Ruth, namely, land property and human property are one and the same: "The day you acquire the field from the hand of Naomi, you are also acquiring Ruth the Moabites" (Ruth 4:5). While the bare facts of this reading are accurate, it misses another line of emphasis in the story—namely, that Ruth, like the Lukan woman, is a highly capable and bold agent of her own desires who courageously transgresses social boundaries in order to welcome the body of her lover. She does not define herself as a passive object to be bought and sold; rather, she is an active agent of her desires and hopes.[24]

Consider one example that illustrates the agency and resourcefulness of both women, the kissing woman and Ruth. While the anonymous woman uses what she has at hand—her hair—to care for Jesus' body, so also does Ruth rely on her own assets—in this case, her rhetorical skills—to claim Boaz as her kinsman, even though she had a nearer kinsman (unnamed in the story, Ruth 3:12-13) who should have been her more likely partner. Like the Lukan woman who follows through on her desires for Jesus, Ruth prefers Boaz and goes after him, not her closer cousin. In both cases, eros's arrow follows its own logic.

The role Boaz's "feet" play in the account further illuminates the narrative artistry at work in the Lukan story. Readers of Ruth have long understood Ruth's action of uncovering Boaz's feet as another way of speaking about sex. With the exception of Song of Solomon, in general the Bible does not use explicit language to describe sexual activity or genitalia but relies instead on pointed, conventional euphemisms to communicate these ideas (e.g., "loins" or "feet" for genitalia, "nakedness" or "knowing" for sexual union).[25] In light of these stylistic devices, new vistas of meaning are opened in Luke 7 when this narrative is read against the backdrop of the Book of Ruth. As Hornsby writes,

> Luke's heightened attention to the feet of Jesus may also suggest to readers various sexual images. That "feet" is a euphemism for male genitals not only in Hebrew texts but also in the Septuagint as well as other Hellenistic and Greco-Roman literature has been convincingly argued. Chapter 3 of the book of Ruth, a plausible intertext to Luke's pericope, offers one of the strongest examples of

the euphemism. . . . I am not arguing that Luke presents
the anointing woman as attending to Jesus' genitals; I am
merely suggesting that to any reader, first century or present day, familiar with the book of Ruth, Luke's attention
to a woman at a man's feet sexually nuances a narrative
that portrays a woman in an active role.[26]

Ruth's story and Luke's text can be read as tender portraits of
warm-hearted *haptology* (Gk. touching). Beyond the taboos
and prohibitions of their respective cultures, both narratives
are about hands touching "feet," arousing the appreciation
of the men who are the partners in their erotic adventures,
and climaxing in enriched experiences of God's presence and
power (i.e., the preservation of the Davidic line in Ruth, and
the forgiveness of the woman's sins in Luke). Just as Luke's
unnamed woman ceaselessly kisses Jesus' feet and makes real
possibilities of carnal intimacy that shatter the prohibitions
concerning public space and public familiarity in antiquity, so
also Ruth may be seen as following her heart's yearnings and
actively shaping her relationship with Boaz, shattering post-
exilic Israel's definition of women as chattel.

Toni Morrison's Gospel of Flesh

Toni Morrison's novel *Beloved*, published in 1987, is a gripping
fictional retelling of the true story of the infanticide of a little
girl by her grief-stricken mother in 1850. Sethe, the protago-
nist of the novel, is a runaway slave who is almost recaptured,
along with her children, at a time when escaped slaves could
be hunted like animals across state lines and taken into cus-
tody by their masters or bounty hunters. Sethe kills one of her

daughters, the "crawling-already? girl" Beloved—so the title
of the novel—in a frantic attempt to prevent her from being
returned to slavery by her nemesis, Schoolteacher. In part, the
novel is a series of flashbacks to the antebellum and Civil War
years in which Sethe, now with her other daughter, Denver,
is haunted by the unspeakable memories of Beloved's death
and related events at the Sweet Home plantation where she
was housed. Sethe's good friend from the Sweet Home years,
Paul D, comes to live with her, Denver, and Beloved, the half-
woman, half-child ghost of the infant Sethe killed earlier. Sethe
remembers how Schoolteacher's plantation boys assaulted her
at Sweet Home, stole her breast milk, and cut open her back
with beatings; and Paul D recalls life on the chain gang and
the humiliation of wearing a horse's bit in his mouth, contort-
ing his face into a painful grimace.

Beloved tells a story of indescribable physical suffering, on
the one hand, and of bodies being healed through hair-comb-
ing, back-touching, breast-feeding, foot-rubbing and hand-
holding, on the other. Readers encounter bodies that are broken
beyond repair and souls crushed without mercy or remorse.
Healing seems impossible, but Morrison uses spirituality—a
certain kind of African-derived, body-loving, nature-based religion—as the medicine the slaves and ex-slaves in the novel
employ to heal themselves. In particular, she profiles Baby
Suggs, Sethe's mother-in-law and itinerant evangelist, whose
message, as Valerie Smith writes, "which transforms the Christian message of self-abnegation and deliverance after death, is
meant to heal the broken and suffering bodies of those who
endured slavery."[27] Nine years after Baby Suggs's death, Sethe
remembers her sermons and dancing in the Clearing, an open
space deep in the woods outside Cincinnati where slaves and

fugitives would gather to hear Baby Suggs, sitting on a large rock in the trees, preach her new gospel of flesh:

> "Here," she said, "in this here place, we flesh; flesh that weeps, laughs; flesh that dances on bare feet in grass. Love it. Love it hard. Yonder they do not love your flesh. They despise it. They don't love your eyes; they'd just as soon pick em out. No more do they love the skin on your back. Yonder they flay it. And O my people they do not love your hands. Those they only use, tie, bind, chop off and leave empty! Love them. Raise them up and kiss them. Touch others with them, pat them together, stroke them on your face 'cause they don't love that either. You got to love it, you! . . . . This is flesh I'm talking about here. Flesh that needs to be loved. Feet that need to rest and to dance; backs that need support; shoulders that need arms, strong arms I'm telling you."[28]

Sethe recalls Baby Suggs's healing services as "fixing ceremonies" that enable her to recover—somewhat—from the physical and psychological wounds suffered under slavery and its aftermatch. Sethe's broken recovery sets the stage for readers today to mend from the toxic effects caused by the transatlantic slave system in its time and other systems of oppression in our own time. Baby Suggs's sermons in the Clearing allow present-day readers to regard the whole novel itself as an extended fixing ceremony—"a prayer," as Barbara Christian writes, "a ritual grounded in active remembering which might result, first of all, in our understanding why it is that so many of us are wounded, fragmented, and in a state of longing. Then, perhaps, we might move beyond that fracturing to those actions that might result in communal healing and in a rede-signing of the contemporary world called the 'New World.'"[29] This sort of "spiritual" reading of Beloved—but spiritual in the sense of world-affirming, not world-denying—is a counter-per-formance that staves off the debilitating effects of pathological, anticorporeal religion. In its worst moments, Christianity, and its antebellum henchmen, despise the flesh, but Baby Suggs teaches us to love our flesh. They tell us to hate our bodies, but she tells us to raise up and kiss and tenderly touch our bodies, and others' bodies as well. Baby Suggs's gospel of flesh is a fixing ceremony that grounds readers' desires to per-form rituals of healing and renewal in the face of institutional systems, including the Christian church, that inculcate disgust and derision toward this beautifully enfleshed world, God's gift to all of us and to ourselves.

In the novel's chronology, Sethe has another healing encounter with Paul D around the time of Baby Suggs's min-istry in the Clearing. She tells Paul D the chilling story of the Sweet Home assault, when the plantation boys extracted Sethe's breast milk and then whipped her after she com-plained to Mrs. Garner, mute and powerless, the proprietress of Sweet Home (so named, horrifically and ironically). She says "Schoolteacher made one [of the boys] open up my back, and when it closed it made a tree. It grows there still."[30] Sethe says this as she is bending over a hot stove, at which point Paul D reaches

> behind her, bending down, his body an arc of kindness,
> he held her breasts in the palms of his hands. He rubbed
> his cheek on her back and learned that way her sor-
> row, the roots of it; its wide trunk and intricate branches.

Raising his fingers to the hooks of her dress, he knew without seeing them or hearing any sigh that the tears were coming fast. And when the top of her dress was around her hips and he saw the sculpture her back had become, like the decorative work of an ironsmith too passionate for display, he could think but not say, "Aw, Lord, girl." And he would tolerate no peace until he had touched every ridge and leaf of it with his mouth, none of which Sethe could feel because her back skin had been dead for years. What she knew was that the responsibility for her breasts, at last, was in somebody else's hands.[31]

Sethe and Paul D's love story is a sensual tale of renewal and pleasure that counterbalances the scenes of unbearable cruelty in the novel. Paul D's hands are an artist's painting a work of beauty over a canvas of flesh crying out for life and deliverance. Sethe's breasts have come home, nestled in the hollows of Paul D's hands, hands that show her that the care of her breasts, at last, are in someone else's hands, and breasts that show him the delight and wonder of intimacy with a woman of fortitude and passion. When Paul D thinks, but cannot say, "Aw, Lord, girl," he and Sethe are making a nest for God to inhabit, a beautiful place for the Spirit to indwell, a setting where the Lord—"Aw, Lord, girl"—is present and alive and beating in the rhythm of the two hearts that are now one, the two bodies that are now one flesh. Erotically charged, sexually inflected, this scene, like the scene of Baby Suggs in the Clearing, offers readers a fixing ceremony, a gospel of flesh, that they can enter into for their own restoration and repair.

Biblical Haptology for Our Time

The scandal of Luke's narrative of the woman who loved too much is that a certain type of woman had the temerity to violate sacrosanct boundaries of appropriate public conduct by touching (*haptos*) and kissing (*kataphileo*) Jesus. The "tell"—the exegetical hint to the reader—that reveals the thrust of the story is Simon's comment *sotto voce* that if Jesus were a prophet then he would know what sort of woman this is and, by implication, not allow her to touch him. However, Jesus not only permits the woman's touches and kisses, he relishes in them. Indeed, he luxuriates in them to the point of upbraiding, and likely humiliating, Simon and his guests by honoring the woman as a lover—his lover?—a woman who shows to everyone what real hospitality, even affection, is. Quiet at first as she wets and wipes his feet with her tears and hair, Jesus eventually speaks and offers to forgive the woman her sins and offers her God's peace. Wetting, wiping, kissing, anointing, touching—this courageous woman from the city, like Ruth and Sethe, has presumably suffered greatly and is now transforming her suffering by seeking carnal joy in her beloved. The Lukan woman, Ruth, and Sethe self-actualize by seeking pleasure and healing in the face of large-scale structures of social and political subjugation. In these transgressive performances of desire and love, God becomes real and is made present to the actors and their readers alike.

Friedrich Nietzsche lamented that Christianity's greatest sin is to despise life, drive underground one's innermost drives and passions, and teach contempt for the body.[32] But in the cracks and along the margins of Christianity's erstwhile ambivalence and sometimes hostility toward sensual pleasure there emerges many extraordinary celebrations of erotic delight and embodied existence in scripture and elsewhere. Christianity will always be in travail with itself, but might it be possible one day that the gospel of flesh would trump the Christian ideal of sexual renunciation? Biblical stories and modern fiction alike offer an antidote to so much *contemptus corporis* nonsense in the annals of official Christian teaching. The logic and scandal of Christian faith has always been an exercise in the coincidence of opposites (that is, divinity and humanity are one). This book calls on people of faith to recover this ancient incarnational wisdom and renew the unity of spirit and flesh, the sacred and the body, God and humankind so that physical, erotic, sexual life can become a privileged site of divine power and love once again.

Chapter Four

EAT WELL
(SEEK JUSTICE)

"In this plate of food,
I see the entire universe
supporting my existence."—Thich Nhat Hanh[1]

In the previous chapter, I read the story of Jesus and the Lukan woman as a lavish display of unbounded affection and intimacy. I offered the story as a model of unity between spirit and flesh, where pleasure and longing are celebrated as God's good gifts rather than disparaged as inimical to religious life. Celebrating the goodness of erotic desire in the last chapter is complemented by this chapter's focus on good, nutritious food as God's ideal as well. My thesis is that health and well-being of the whole body—in sexual expression and diet alike—form the basis of the passionate struggle to save Earth for future generations. Love of flesh in its many forms is the bedrock value that liberates our desires to live compassionately and sustainably within our lush and verdant planet home.

Under the rubric of green Christianity, and with special reference to the blighted city of Chester, Pennsylvania, I argue that lack of access to affordable, nourishing food is an environmental justice problem embedded within a host of other social and economic problems. A holistic analysis of the dysfunctional web that ties together seemingly disparate social pathologies can make sense of, and provide solutions for, the ecocrisis, including the food crisis, in urban communities today. The quest for ecojustice, food security, and sustainable living in disadvantaged areas is inextricably linked, for example, to the need for good schools and systemic workforce development. This quest only makes sense in relation to a deeper understanding of the historic, economic, and political forces that have fueled the crisis. In this chapter I offer a case study of a grocery co-op in Chester as a successful experiment in sustainable food justice and participatory democracy that directly confronts the urban crisis, including the rising incidence of obesity and diabetes in under-resourced communities.

By avoiding over reliance on the carbon-intensive regime of Big Food, the Co-op is a living parable of how local food choices can undergird the health of consumers as well as the biosystems that support this and future generations of animals and plants. I conclude that the powers of resurrection hope and biblical justice are compelling resources for combatting the mean-spirited politics of greed and power that drive the downward cycle of American cities today.

The Dream and the Nightmare

"Mark! Do you want these asparagus? If you don't take them, they'll go bad," said Tina Johnson. "Sure," I replied, knowing that the asparagus had already endured a final round of weekly sales activity and, without refrigeration, probably would not last another week. It was the end of my volunteer shift as a cashier on a recent Saturday morning at Chester's Community Grocery Co-op, a start-up produce market in Chester, a downtrodden post-industrial city of 35,000 people, just west of Philadelphia.[2] The Chester Co-op is an experiment in food democracy and sustainable living in which Tina Johnson, Co-op director, purchases wholesale fruit and vegetables, much of it locally grown, and then retails her goods twice weekly in a former jazz club in downtown Chester (the Co-op cannot afford its own building). It is the only grocery store in Chester because the large supermarket chains have redlined the city as too big a financial risk.

In poor, minority communities awash in chronic environmental and health problems, services like the Co-op are a lifeline for residents for whom fresh, affordable food is not easily attainable. In these settings, environmental justice means food

security, that is, ready access to reasonably priced and nutritious food for healthy living. And it means that Chesterites
partner with local farmers to support regional food production
without relying on the fuel-intensive and land-depleting practices within the globalized food economy. Through buying
local food and avoiding reliance on ecologically destructive
industrialized agriculture, the Co-op is an exercise in "agricultural sustainability" by "meeting the present and future needs
of all people for food and health while caring for their natural
and social environment."[3] This local store increases Chester's
social capital by uniting the city around good eating, but it
lacks the financial capital to support fully its mission. Without
a steady source of income, the Co-op must purchase foodstuffs
each week on the basis of what it sold the week before. It cannot afford the basic trappings of most grocery stores: shelving,
signage, carts, even refrigeration. Without refrigeration, a lot
of produce quickly spoils. So on a recent spring morning, after
a good day of strong sales, I was happy to take home some
leftover asparagus at the end of my shift but also sadly aware
that an enterprise so vital to the health of the community is so
marginal that it cannot afford to bind over week-to-week its
principal product, fresh produce.

My point in this chapter is that many inner-city communities' lack of access to good food is an environmental justice
problem embedded within a host of other social and economic
problems. Only a holistic analysis of the systemic forces that tie
together seemingly disconnected social pathologies can make
sense of, and provide solutions for, the ecocrisis in urban communities today. The quest for ecojustice and sustainable living
in blighted communities is inextricably linked, for example, to
the need for good schools and workforce development, among

other important issues. In that nexus, Chester has become a poster child for small U.S. cities that have all the problems of big city life with few of the resources to tackle them. The quest for sustainable ecojustice in Chester—and other inner-city communities—only makes sense in relation to a deeper understanding of the historic, economic, and political forces that have fueled the crisis.

In Chester, the American dream has failed for struggling individuals and families mired in failing schools, dangerous environmental conditions, and low-paying, dead-end jobs—or no jobs at all.[4] But I and others live in hope that the city's dire conditions will change. The ground of my volunteer activism—resurrection hope—is best captured in a newly painted Chester wall mural *(reproduced here)* where a little girl with a crown of thorns on her head is reaching out to the viewer with a dove of peace in one hand, and a protest sign in the other. Local residents and children, and students from Swarthmore College, where I teach, created this mural in 2006.[5] The girl is a visual metaphor of Chester. Like Jesus, she wears a crown of thorns, symbolizing how the city has suffered through unemployment, disinvestment, and broken schools—the collapse of the city's core social infrastructure. But the small protest sign the girl carries in her left hand stands for the city's resistance to these forces of oppression, and the dove in her right represents Chester's hope that a depressed population will again enjoy peace and prosperity in the future. The mural animates my expectation that Chester, left for dead, can rise again in new life.

My idea of resurrection hope is borrowed from German theologian Jürgen Moltmann's theology of hope. For Moltmann, healthy Christian belief grounds action toward fulfilling the promise—always provisional and fragmentary—that justice and peace will become the norm on Earth. "The hope of resurrection must bring about a new understanding of the world," writes Moltmann, "the world of possibilities, the world in which we can serve the future, promised truth of righteousness and peace."[6] Glossing Moltmann, resurrection hope is the fiery nucleus at the center of my life. It is the basis of my conviction that the demons of grinding poverty and joblessness can be conquered, that good schools and safe neighborhoods can take root and flourish, and that political hacks and corrupt officials can be pushed aside and in some cases punished for their crimes against local residents. Like the girl in the mural, I believe that Chester, crucified, will rise again into a new future.

At present, Chester is known primarily as a poverty-stricken city that survives on the fringes of America's global economic dominance. Dr. Martin Luther King Jr. did pastoral training and received his ministerial degree from Crozer Theological Seminary in Chester in the early 1950s. Continuing King's legacy, it is a place of strong families, gifted young people, committed churches and mosques, and visionary leaders who care deeply about the city's future. But its heyday as a pre-war industrial metropolis under the slogan "What Chester makes, makes Chester" has long since passed with the collapse of the good manufacturing jobs that were at its economic base. Today its average household income is $24,000 per year, its unemployment rate hovers around 30 percent, only 30 percent of adults have a high school diploma or equivalent, its violent crime rate is two to three times the national average, and it has the highest infant mortality rate in the state. Many of Chester's residents now inhabit the ranks of the dispossessed—the forgotten leftovers of the American dream who do not have access to the good schools, workforce development, clean environments, and quality health care that many others of us consider our birthrights.

Four years ago I forged a covenant relationship with clergy and activists in Chester and the nearby town of Swarthmore, where I live and work. I had heard about some of Chester's urban prophets, and I wanted to be part of the transformation and hope that these agents for change were bringing to the city. At that time I helped to organize the Chester Swarthmore Learning Institute to advance political change and social transformation within our respective communities. Chester is a gritty urban community. Swarthmore is a leafy green college town. My Chester colleagues and I have crossed racial and cultural divisions in order to make our institute work. This has not been easy. Mistakes have been made and misunderstandings have arisen. But I believe real change happens when people from different walks of life come together in common purpose and trust to see how they can mutually strengthen the well-being of others. My life has been transformed through my partnership with friends in Chester. In turn, I hope that these friends and the communities they serve have also been enriched through our association.

Hope amidst Despair

The central message of the Christian gospel is straightforward: follow Jesus by commiting oneself to radical personal and social transformation. St. Paul writes in the Book of Philippians: "Let the same mind be in you that was in Christ Jesus, who, though he was in the form of God, emptied himself, taking the form of a slave, and became obedient to the point of death—even death on a cross. Therefore God also highly

exalted him" (2:5-9). This is the model all disciples of Jesus
are to follow: be like Jesus, who emptied himself, became a
servant (slave), suffered death, and was raised up (exalted).
The Christian way is to follow Jesus through self-emptying
and resurrection hope. Self-emptying is abandoning narrow
self-gratification in order to serve the interests of others. Resurrection hope is the confidence that God is able to raise up
everyday people to revolutionize systemically distorted structures, no matter how hopeless and entrenched these structures
might appear to be. Such hope is impossibly expectant that life
can emerge from death—that new beginnings can be generated out of the detritus of broken dreams. No matter how bad
things get, even in the moment of death, God is able to create
new life under the direst social conditions.

I cannot work in Chester without such hope. For me, the
dysfunction is too deeply entrenched, the pain and suffering too longstanding to be overcome otherwise. Resurrection
hope propels me toward a sustainable and robust commitment to the well-being of my Chester neighbors; it carries me
through the crushing disappointments and spiritual assaults
that come with such work. This hope is not layered onto
an already existing social commitment; it does not provide a
religious patina to a preformed political agenda. This hope,
rather, is the genesis of my politics as such. It is this hope
itself that is the wellspring of my long-term commitment and
enthusiasm for this work.

Tragically, Christians are notorious for translating the language of hope into vapid pie-in-the-sky foolishness. Antebellum white ministers were infamous for telling African slaves
that the object of Christian hope is not changed social conditions in *this* world, but blissful existence in the world *beyond*.[7]

Today as well, many clergy counsel the faithful to avoid large-scale justice movements in favor of personal salvation and morality. But this type of politically indifferent, otherworldly religion is a Christian heresy.[8] It has nothing to do with the religion of Jesus. Indeed, it is a betrayal of everything that Jesus taught and did. At the inauguration of his public ministry in the Gospel of Luke, Jesus quotes the Book of Isaiah saying, "The Spirit of the Lord is upon me to bring good news to the poor, proclaim release to the captives, recovery of sight to the blind, and to let the oppressed go free" (4:18-19). Remembering Paul's mandate to have the mind of Christ, the real Christian message is clear: be like Jesus through solidarity with the poor, the incarcerated, the disabled, and all others who are oppressed in any way. This revolutionary social theme is the essential thread that ties together the whole Bible

In spite of the promising history and basic goodness of Chester residents, how did things get so bad? As in many blighted, drug-infested areas, the social and economic fabric of Chester has been shredded by three equally powerful forces: toxic education, ecological violence, and poverty pimping.

Losing a Generation of Children

Chester's schools are among the worst in Pennsylvania. City residents have the lowest literacy rate in the state, and the school district is consistently ranked 499 or 500 among the five hundred school systems in Pennsylvania, according to standardized test scores.[9] Until recently, the school district was managed by a for-profit "education" vendor that propelled the schools' downward slide toward low test scores, chronic absenteeism, and occasional shootings and riots on school grounds. Then, through early 2007, it was run by a politically appointed part-time overseer with a track record of financial misconduct and political cronyism. The result is that most students from grades one through twelve cannot read at grade level, the high school dropout rate is 50 percent, and almost as many high school students commit crimes and become incarcerated as graduate and go to college (about 5–6 percent in both cases).[10]

As one superintendent recently put it, "My school is a pipeline to prison right now. When you lose more than 50 percent of your children to the streets in four years, where else are they going? And many of them do go right to prison."[11] Chester schools have become educationally and personally debilitating for scores of students. One teen recently told a Swarthmore student of mine that all of the students in one of his classes had been kicked out of school for a week because a classmate had thrown a paper airplane during a lesson.

But there is hope amidst the despair. Both the for-profit school manager and the corrupt overseer have been thrown out in favor of a new state-appointed oversight board. The community worked tirelessly to bring down the previous manager and overseer and is guardedly optimistic that the new school board will move away from the "plantation" management style of the past to fully incorporating the voices and interests of teachers, parents, and children in the decision-making process. Enabling local stakeholders to be active participants in shaping the future of their schools is the key to urban renewal today. Continually fueled by resurrection hope, I partner with local clergy and community leaders to insist upon accountability from school officials, and I provide Swarthmore College students as after-school mentors and tutors for Chester young people. My and

my colleagues' intervention in the school district is designed
to tear out the poisoned roots of mismanagement, influence-
peddling, and cynicism that characterize this system. With the
ouster of the preceding top officials, many of us believe a new
day dawns for genuine educational reform in Chester.

Dumping on the Poor

Chester's environmental crisis is a twofold problem that stems
from chronic poverty. On the one hand, food security looms
large in impoverished neighborhoods, where groceries must
be bought on the cheap. On the other, the degradation of
Chester's physical environment is now firmly established
because its economy is partially dependent on the for-profit
management of toxic wastes within the city. In economically
distressed communities, the waste industry's assurances of
a stabilized tax base and jobs for unemployed residents are
impossible to resist.[12] But what is the real cost of such promises? Four waste treatment facilities now make Chester their
home: a sewage treatment plant, a metal-recycling plant, a
regional incinerator, and a medical-waste autoclave (currently
not operating). The clustering of waste industries only a few
yards from residential areas has brought about an infestation
of rodents, noxious odors, the presence of hundreds of trucks
each day at all hours in the neighborhood, and toxic air emissions that have contributed to lead poisoning and have raised
the specter of cancer to two-and-a-half times greater than the
average risk for other area residents.[13]

Predominantly African American, Chester is a stunning
instance of environmental racism. The inequitable distribu-
tion of biohazards in a city where the majority population is

black and economically distressed identifies Chester as one of the country's worst examples of environmental apartheid. It has become one of metro Philadelphia's toxic sacrifice zones, where waste from surrounding affluent, white municipalities is disproportionately dumped in the vain hope that such dumping will revitalize the city's economic fortunes. But as the former mayor of Chester put it, many people do not want to live and work in a city known as a toxic "killing field": "Chester should not and will not serve as a dumping ground. A dumping ground for what no other borough, no other township, or no other city will accept. Yes, Chester needs the taxes, Chester needs the jobs. But, Chester also needs to improve its image and not be a killing field."[14]

Resurrection hope propels me and other area residents to resist the imposition of environmental hazards on Chester. My faith in Jesus' resurrection from death sustains my long battles against eco-injustice. We march in the streets, meet with community officials, and attend regulatory hearings to fight against toxic racism. I hang my hope on the slim reed of occasional victories against the eco-domination system. Indeed, in recent years, at the urging of local citizens, the state did not approve the siting of a soil treatment plant, a local paper mill was not allowed to burn tires for fuel, a biotech firm that would have increased overall pollution in the area was kept out, and the sewage treatment plant was successfully sued by nearby residents for violating federal and state air and water pollution laws. Still, the waste facilities in the killing fields of Chester continue to operate. We live in hope that the corrupt regime of unequal waste management will end. Hope never fully realized is not hope destroyed, however, and so the battle for justice against the big industrial polluters rages on.

Gambling and the Oppressed

Chester boasts a spectacular waterfront on its southern border facing the Delaware River, just west of Philadelphia. The waterfront used to be home to shipbuilding and manufacturing jobs. As in much of the United States, this industrial base collapsed two generations ago, rendering the waterfront a wasteland of empty factories and crumbling infrastructure. Since that time, the waterfront has become a zone of economic opportunity— attracting, among other industries, a casino—with the promise of making lots of tax-free money for developers, since new businesses in such zones are exempt from property taxes until 2013. Instead of measurable commitments to workforce development as a prerequisite for setting up shop, however, the new casino and other developers are grabbing up valuable riverfront real estate for pennies on the dollar and offering little to local workers in exchange.[15]

A group of community activists and clergy have formed the Fair Deal Coalition to pressure city government and the casino to allocate substantial gaming profits to education and job training. This is necessary to finance the workforce- and skills-development necessary for Chester's poor to compete in the economic boom that the new waterfront growth promises. But in light of the city's poverty and broken schools, the economic benefits of the casino will not flow toward residents without a focused effort to train and employ its underserved population. As the Fair Deal Coalition puts it, "There seems to be an assumption on the part of proponents of legalized gambling that the injection of new capital into the local economy, regardless of where it enters the system, will eventually trickle down to those at the bottom. We find this to be a highly dubious assumption, especially in a community where so many residents lack the training and skill to compete in the job market."[16] Chester's new economic order will be built at the expense of low-income, minority residents unless city officials can be persuaded to redirect these funds toward long-term sustainable economic development for disadvantaged residents.

Studies show that economic opportunity and quality of life are generally undermined by gambling development.[17] While big profits go to the corporations that run such enterprises, future analyses will likely show that Chester's casino has introduced more crime, gaming addiction, bankruptcy, and family disruption into the city—an inevitable byproduct of gambling in blighted communities. Further shredding of the city's social fabric will continue the endemic practice of poverty pimping (producing profits at the expense of the poor) that is rampant in Chester. To date, the casino and other new ventures have generated millions of dollars in tax revenues, but the bulk of these funds go to the state and surrounding county, and what *does* go back to the city is being used for debt relief and similar municipal activities instead of being the basis for a sustained and focused investment in the city's human capital. But resurrection hope animates the struggle to incorporate the disenfranchised in the long-awaited economic revival of the city. To this end, the Fair Deal Coalition is a bright star in the dim universe of chronic poverty and unemployment.

A Case Study of Resurrection Hope

In recent years a new environmental problem has confronted communities such as Chester: epidemic levels of obesity and diabetes among both adult and child populations. At one time, poor diets in urban areas led to underweight residents. Today, poverty and food insecurity mean more Americans are becoming overweight, and suffering from related diseases, by relying on added high-fat and high-sugar diets. The alarming rise in obesity rates is evident in body mass measurement data since the 1960s. By the year 2000, 65 percent of the adult U.S. population was overweight, and the climb in obesity among children has been even more alarming. As one study puts it, "In the 1960's approximately 5 percent of children in the U.S. were overweight. By the 1990's the percentage of overweight children had more than doubled, and currently over 15 percent of children and adolescents aged 6-19 are overweight. Even more concerning, 10 percent of preschoolers aged 2-5 are overweight."[18]

Socially, overweight children can experience low self-esteem, poor body image, and isolation from their peers. Medically, serious lifelong disabilities, such as diabetes and cardiovascular disease, can be caused by obesity. Indeed, the surge in cases among children and teens of type-2 diabetes, a metabolic disease in which the body's natural insulin production is disordered, is particularly alarming because type-2 diabetes used to be considered primarily an adult-onset disease.[19] The spike in this type of diabetes is directly linked to the rise in obesity. It has now reached epidemic proportions among children and adolescents, even though it is not a congenital condition and is entirely preventable by eating a healthy diet and getting regular exercise.[20] But the very social conditions that make balanced eating and weekly exercise part of a child's life have rotted away in many underserved, urban settings. Adult caregivers feel pressured and distracted; healthy food options are limited and often expensive; and leisure time, especially in neighborhoods with high crime rates where children are at risk of injury, is now more devoted to sedentary media than outdoor games and activities. These factors conspire to keep kids hooked on low-quality, high-fat diets of junk calories and fast food that create the false sensation of having one's hunger satisfied. Obesity and attendant health problems like type-2 diabetes are the ever-growing norm among urban kids in America today.

At first glance, the urban food predicament may not seem like an environmental problem. When we think about "environmentalism," we often think about wilderness preservation work among conservation groups, on the one hand, or battling big polluters in urban settings among justice-seeking antitoxics activists, on the other. But the food security crisis, along with the concomitant health problems it spawns, is just as much an environmental problem as saving forests and wetlands or protecting city neighborhoods from polluters. This too is an environmental justice issue that cries out to be addressed. Yes, it is wrong for waste vendors inequitably to dump and process trash in disempowered cities that have been hoodwinked by the promotional pitch that the waste industry can revitalize these particular areas. But it is just as wrong for supermarket chains—the primary providers, for good and for ill, of basic nutrition for most Americans—to redline a whole city by declaring it off-limits to grocery store investment. In the case of the waste industry *and* the food industry, the real driving force in corporate decision-making about where and whether to develop a particular venture is obeisance to the god of the market. Market forces dictate what development can and cannot take place in America's struggling cities. Many of us still operate with a residual belief that the government's legal apparatus should be pressed into the service of ensuring

education and health coverage for most citizens, and especially children. But many Americans do not think that clean
ecosystems, or access to good food, is a natural right. For this
reason, I think the ecojustice crisis today is twofold: it stems
from the dangerous clustering of biohazards in communities
already suffering from ill health, and it consists of the total
absence, as in the case of Chester, of any viable food sources
to nourish city dwellers, which of course only further degrades
the well-being of such communities.

The Chester Co-op is a beacon of light and hope on a
landscape pockmarked with poverty, toxic environmental
conditions, schools mired in despair, chronic food insecurity,
and citizens' lack of readiness for the workforce. The Co-op
both *is* and *is not* about food. On the one hand, its mission is
to provide fresh nutritious produce at affordable prices to local
residents by establishing good relations with local farmers to
supply the store. Chester has not had a supermarket for fifteen
years. Residents have had to travel out of town to shop and
many do not have their own transportation for this purpose.
Obesity and diabetes haunt urban neighborhoods cut off from
mainstream retail stores. The Co-op addresses the problem of
food security and the health crisis by relying on an elegantly
simple business model: members own and run the store themselves by selling local food at reduced prices. This approach
keeps prices low, stops the loss of inventory through theft
and spoilage, and generates few administrative overhead costs
because "member-owners" contribute their own sweat equity
to the venture by working in the store three to four hours
per month. They also pay a refundable membership fee of
$200.00, with the option of paying this fee over time on a
graduated basis. The Co-op is an exercise in sustainable food

justice by providing Chesterites with a healthy nutrition option
long after the Big Food stores had abandoned the city as too
risky an investment option.

Yes, the Co-op markets affordable produce, but it has
another mission as well: to develop Chester's own sense of
pride and leadership potential by teaching residents how to
successfully manage a for-profit business. The store sells food
by making a direct investment in human capital. As well, urban-
rural ties to area farms are strengthened. The Co-op provides
food access and, just as importantly, it develops residents' life
skills and management potential in a convivial, democratic
work environment. The store's oversight board and membership meetings are run by local folk, many of whom have never
held positions of responsibility. At a recent meeting, the con-
vener began with the following: "I have never spoken before
a group before and want to thank Tina and the rest of you for
giving me the opportunity to lead this meeting." The meeting
was a big success and we all felt a sense of communal well-
being by witnessing this leadership transformation in one of
our team members.

The emerging field of sustainability economics speaks about
the "triple bottom line" in successful green businesses that are
right for the twenty-first century. Such enterprises not only produce financial capital but they also develop human and environmental capital, through just management-employee relations
and sustainable, low-carbon emitting relations with the natural
world.[21] The Chester Co-op is an ecojustice experiment that has
made healthy nutrition a living option for hard-working urban
dwellers. But it is about more than food. It is a model for how
to run a business where people's needs count first, the urban
health crisis is addressed, and local relations with nearby family

farms are developed and strengthened. In such models, participants' economic needs are met alongside their development as community leaders in a just and sustainable world.

The Joy of Resistance

"When Jesus calls a person, he bids him 'come and die.'" Dietrich Bonhoeffer, the Lutheran theologian and martyr who joined the resistance in an attempt to kill Adolf Hitler, wrote these words in his book *The Cost of Discipleship.* Not all of us are asked to give up our lives, as Bonhoeffer did, to combat systemic evil. But all of us—as people of faith, or no faith at all—are called to sacrifice our private interests to serve a greater good. For most of us, however, such acts are not true sacrifices. Parenting my children, teaching a class, or meeting with Chester activists to generate social change is not a sacrifice, but a joyous and life-sustaining commitment to the well-being of the commons. In these commitments I am no longer an automaton in service of the capitalist machine but a member of a global resistance movement fighting the spreading tentacles of the domination system. Belonging to this movement, I make common cause with all people of good faith. Some of my colleagues in the Chester Swarthmore Institute are prophetic clergy, others are secular activists, but all of us are driven by common visionary sources—Paulo Freire's radical pedagogy, Saul Alinsky's community organizing, Wangari Maathai's environmental activism—that sustain us over the long haul of our respective work challenges in Chester. Together we draw deeply from the religious *and* non-religious wells of our own backgrounds and traditions in order to keep ourselves fresh and alive in the face of continuing adversity.

I am not imperialistic about religion in this regard. I do
not think religion is necessary for social change. While *I* need
the strength of resurrection hope to propel me forward, it is
not necessary to make religion a requirement for sustainable
social action. What is necessary, rather, is to plumb the depths
of one's own life-source—be it ethical, political, religious, or
otherwise—and therein be nurtured, fed, and energized to re-
enter the fray and battle the forces of oppression.

As an ecojustice seeking enterprise, the Chester Co-op
market is an exercise in sustainable agriculture. It provides
an alternative model of healthy food consumption and just
relations with our human and animal neighbors. By avoiding over-reliance on the carbon-intensive regime of Big Food,
the Co-op is a living parable of how local food choices can
support the health of consumers along with the biosystems
that will nourish this and future generations of animals and
plants. Shopping at the store is an investment in bioregional
capital. Its whole grain bread is produced by a local bakery,
its eggplants are harvested down the street through an urban
garden project, its peaches and corn come from nearby farms
in Pennsylvania's Amish country. It makes its contribution to
protecting soil and water resources, ensuring the health of
urban communities and supporting the economic viability of
local farm operations. The Co-op cannot get all of its produce
locally, but it continues to strive to offer shoppers positive
food choices that are not dependent on the high-fat, high-
sugar products the global food system delivers to low-income
families, posing health risks that are now reaching epidemic
proportions.

Today, the Christian gospel has been co-opted by politicians and preachers who trumpet personal morality at the

expense of fighting against the structural conditions that lock down America's underclass in depraved and dehumanizing urban environments. This is a betrayal of the Christian message. The defining feature of Jesus' ministry was solidarity with the poor and oppressed. To be a revolutionary Christian today is to follow in Jesus' steps and care for the marginalized and forgotten in a world hell bent on unsustainable agricultural and economic policies. When despair for the world overwhelms me, the problems of Chester and the wider planet seem impossible to overcome. But then I recall Jesus' life of compassion and liberation—I remember the girl in the mural wearing her crown of thorns and reaching toward me with outstretched hands—and I am empowered to live to fight another day.

Chapter Five

LIVE A VOCATION

Sustainability respects the interdependence of living beings on one another and on their natural environment. Sustainability means operating a business in a way that causes minimal harm to living creatures and that does not deplete but rather restores and enriches the environment.[1]
—Andrew W. Savitz

The Good Life

In this book I have sought to reposition Christian faith as a celebration of environmental integrity and bodily health. My aim is to show how biblically inspired living is rooted in a rich and verdant planet that supports the well-being and many pleasures of fleshly existence. In the previous chapter my focus fell on good eating in the economically degraded city of Chester,

Pennsylvania, where urban food activists are working hard to sell fresh, affordable produce to their neighbors. Healthy nutrition is bedrock for living a whole and balanced lifestyle—what philosophers call "the good life"—grounded on the central ideals of biblical faith. My graduate school teacher, philosopher Paul Ricoeur, wrote that "the 'good life' is, for each of us, the nebulous of ideals and dreams of achievements with regard to which a life is held to be more or less fulfilled or unfulfilled."[2] Ricoeur went on to say that living well is driven by an "ethical intention" directed at care of oneself and others in just and humane workplaces and other establishments. "Let us define 'ethical intention,'" he writes, "as *aiming at the 'good life' with and for others, in just institutions.*"[3] This comment is the animating force that drives this chapter: How does one live the good life, both in practicing self-esteem and showing solicitude for others, in organizational settings that are responsible and fair? More specifically, with reference to the ecocrisis, I ask: In one's private and corporate existence, is it possible to live fully and do business today without degrading Earth's carrying capacity to support life as we know it? Is economic growth possible without destroying the living systems that make our everyday existence possible in the first place? This query is arguably the most important personal and institutional question of our time. In response, I will sketch the outlines of sustainability economics framed to meet this challenge, turn to a meditation on the qualities of the "kenotic" leader as essential to meeting this challenge, and conclude with a case study of a bicycle store in Boston, Massachusetts, as a model of environmental leadership and fair labor practices.

My orienting question is: What would healthy and successful organizational practices look like at a time when great masses of Earth's human, animal, and plant populations are teetering on the brink of collapse? This question presupposes what many of us now recognize, namely, that we are living in an era of economic and environmental despair, when the triple threats of hunger, poverty, and climate change continue apace. The United Nations estimates that about 25,000 people die every day of hunger or hunger-related causes due to severe, structural poverty worldwide. Even in the United States, the richest country in the history of humankind, the poverty rate for minors is the highest in the industrialized world, with nearly 15% of all minors and 30% of African American children living below the poverty threshold. An entirely preventable disease, HIV/AIDS kills more than two million people a year—making it second only to the Black Death as the largest epidemic in history. The death toll from HIV/AIDS is especially high in Africa, where millions have died, leaving multitudes of children orphans and destroying whole communities.

On the environmental front, the news is no better. Jim Hansen, a top climate specialist at NASA, claims we have just ten years to reduce greenhouse gases before global warming reaches an unstoppable tipping point and transforms our natural world into a "totally different planet."[4] While Earth's temperature rose by one degree during the last century, Hansen and others predict that global temperatures will rise by three to ten degrees this century, resulting in widespread melting of artic glaciers and perhaps even the Greenland landmass. This mass melting could then raise sea levels, astonishingly, by one or two feet, or more, causing low-lying shore communities such as the San Francisco Bay Area and lower Manhattan to gradually disappear. Indeed, the current president of the

Maldives—a string of 1,190 islands in the Indian Ocean—now proposes to move 300,000 Maldivians to higher ground—India? Australia?—because of growing evidence that rising waters will soon swamp his country.[5] Hurricane Katrina along the Gulf Coast in 2005 was a particularly ugly example of the confluence of poverty and climate change in our era: the gradual warming of the Gulf of Mexico by one degree in recent years contributed to the conversion of a tropical storm into a killer hurricane, trapping hundreds of poor people in their homes who didn't have the means to escape the disaster. Equally threatening, climate change is contributing to a global die-off of species similar to the last mass extinction event over 65 million years ago, when the great dinosaurs were wiped out. Biologists conservatively estimate that 30,000 plant and animal species are driven to extinction every year—even the polar bear is now proposed as a threatened species.

Not everyone agrees with this dire scenario. Global warming critics chide many climatologists' and geologists' "undue concerns [regarding] destructive manmade global warming . . . and rampant species loss"; such concerns are generating "solutions" to climate crisis that "are unjustifiably costly and of dubious benefit."[6] But the science seems clear: we are living in an objectively apocalyptic situation that cries out for leaders of intelligence, compassion, and vision who can move us beyond narrow self-interest and conventional bottom line thinking to a new model of whole human societies living responsibly within Earth community.[7] This is a tall order, but I believe that sustainable economic practice is the demand of our time. By rethinking economic growth not as an end in itself but as a value that serves the larger ideal of planetary well-being, we have the potential to move our local and global economies toward an environmentally honest future in which the real costs of our business practices are noted and acted upon.

The Triple Bottom Line

This chapter is a call to institutional sustainability—the development of fiscally solid business practices that fully account for their social and environmental impacts by ensuring that future generations can meet their vital needs in a just and biologically rich world.[8] Andrew Savitz puts it this way:

> Sustainability respects the interdependence of living beings on one another and on their natural environment. Sustainability means operating a business in a way that causes minimal harm to living creatures and that does not deplete but rather restores and enriches the environment.
>
> Sustainability also respects the interdependence of differing aspects of human existence. Economic growth and financial success are important and provide significant benefits to individuals and society as a whole. But other human values are also important, including family life, intellectual growth, artistic expression, and moral and spiritual development. Sustainability means operating a business so as to grow and earn profit while recognizing and supporting the economic and noneconomic aspirations of people both inside and outside the organization on whom the corporation depends.
>
> The only way to succeed in today's interdependent world is to embrace sustainability. Doing so requires companies to identify a wide range of stakeholders to

whom they may be accountable, develop open relationships with them, and finds ways to work with them for
mutual benefit. In the long run, this will create more
profit for the company and more social, economic, and
environmental prosperity for society.[9]

Sustainability is a proleptic category that focuses on the
long-term viability of working business models. It encom-
passes the well-being of workers and consumers in a verdant
world, where all of Earth's inhabitants are deserving of nurture and protection. It asks: How can companies today secure
and manage the labor and environmental resources necessary for achieving their economic goals while also preserving
the capacity of future human communities and ecosystems to
survive and flourish? Native American folklore often speaks
of animal and related resource management practices done
with an eye toward their impact on the seventh generation to
come. Products and services alone are not a true measure of
value; rather, companies must calculate the real cost of doing
business that relies on nature's bounty in the production of
goods and services. Seventh-generation full-cost business and
accounting practices relocate the goal of financial profitability within the context of responsible consumption of energy,
careful management of waste, attention to air and water quality, fair labor practices, and commitment to the well-being of
human society and natural habitats in general.

The seventh-generation ideal is often referred to today as
the *triple bottom line business model* (people, planet, profits).
In this model, financial profits depend upon carefully managed environmental and social performance; corporate, societal, and ecological interests dynamically interact and mutually

support one another. Triple bottom line business practices that measure long-term growth as an increase in financial, natural, and social capital do not, however, simply slap ecosocial responsibility onto a capitalist model as a way of adding "social service" to its list of charitable activities. Triple bottom line— or sustainable—businesses, rather, are seeking to transform capitalism and render it inherently responsive to the exigencies of just labor laws and global climate change, to cite two examples, if they are going to be truly successful, in economic *and* ethical terms, in the competitive global marketplace.[10]

Ironically, many organizations are now discovering that their business model is actually *strengthened* by systematic attention to their contribution to long-term human and ecosystem well-being. Shifting energy use to renewables, reducing or eliminating hazardous wastes, creating products from recycled materials—these steps cut costs in the long run, improve workforce conditions, and minimize environmental impacts. Today the list of triple bottom line companies continues to grow: Toyota's sustainable business practices and high mileage hybrid vehicles, Subway's integral focus on healthy nutrition and civic engagement, Herman Miller's recycling efforts and policy of paying higher prices for sustainably logged timber, and Tom's of Maine's environmentally friendly products and corporate volunteerism. These pro-labor, community-outreach, green businesses did not first become profitable and then later add to their organizational model fair labor and sound environmental practices; rather, sustainability and profitability have been integral to their identity and mission since their founding.

In this regard, take the example of Seeing Things Whole, a productive and visionary national organization of business leaders with moral and religious commitments who argue that the workplace should be reconceived as a center of humane values. At first glance, Seeing Things Whole looks like a large group network committed to sustainability. It enables corporate leaders to examine how the dynamics of organizational structure (identity), animating mission (purpose), and business viability (stewardship) symbiotically interrelate in the life of an institution to promote personal and social transformation. But while Seeing Things Whole does make some ad hoc allusions to sustainability ("Do we operate in ways that honor the human and natural communities which host us?"), these occasional references are belied by a human centered worldview that refers to the human community as the primary stakeholder or center of value in corporate decision-making. Consider how when Seeing Things Whole identifies typical stakeholders, it does so, under its identity rubric, in terms of staff; under its purpose rubric, it discusses clients and suppliers; and under its stewardship rubric, management and trustees.[11] In my judgment, however, "stakeholder" refers to any person, or nonhuman life-form, who is directly or indirectly shaped and determined by the actions of the firm in question. From this perspective, the primary stakeholder in any organizational enterprise is the *entire biotic and abiotic order of the natural world*—Earth's common life-support system—without which particular organizational efforts are not possible. As John Todd and Nancy Jack Todd argue:

> The innumerable and life-endangering environmental ills that currently plague us are the byproducts of human cultures and technologies deeply estranged from the great natural systems of the planet. These same systems are,

ironically, the very processes that ultimately sustain us. Edward Wilson has calculated that humans are destroying species at an extraordinary rate and that between twenty and fifty percent of present living species will be extinct by the year 2025. The only lasting solution to counter this dynamic is to recreate consciously symbiotic relationships between humanity and nature. Such relationships demand nothing less than a fundamental technological revolution designed to integrate advanced societies with the natural world.[12]

Free and open organizational cultures radically depend on diverse and vigorous natural systems for their very survival and longevity. We are "deeply estranged from the great natural systems of the planet," as Todd and Jack Todd argue, and yet "these same systems are, ironically, the very processes that ultimately sustain us."[13] Positive workforce cultures, in which democratic decision-making is a regular feature of management and staff relations is an important step on the path to sustainability. But merely to make this move is not a full embrace of triple bottom line, sustainable business practice. Without clean air, potable water, healthy land-management, and biodiverse plant and animal life—and without these ecological values as front and center of a particular business model—all forms of otherwise laudatory egalitarian institutional life are baseless. Like Seeing Things Whole, corporations now stand at the intersection between *creation-based*, to speak in theological terms, and *person-based* institutional models. Will such corporations remain wedded to an *anthropocentric* organizational structure that makes only passing reference to sustainability, or can they relocate themselves on the *planetary* foundation of biological fecundity and the well-being of all of God's creatures, human and nonhuman alike?

Kenotic Leadership

Before I look further at my call for a shift from anthropocentric to biocentric models of institutional life, I want to pursue analysis of *the quality of persons' inner life* within organizational leadership theory today. Here I shift my focus from the outward issue of sustainability as the core value that should invigorate corporate cultures to the inward issue of the interior qualities of radical self-giving and risk taking that define the leadership of successful organizations. Of course, the outward/inward foci mutually depend upon and reinforce one another: an authentically sustainable business relies upon the character and convictions of its leadership, and in turn attention to the inner life is shaped and supported by triple bottom line institutional settings.

Genuinely effective leadership in the global marketplace relies on a sense of sacred calling rooted in the practice of the inner life. Parker Palmer writes that "the power of authentic leadership is found not in external arrangements but in the human heart. Authentic leaders in every setting—from families to nation-states—aim at liberating the heart, their own and others', so that its powers can liberate the world."[14] The innermost life of the spirit—a power that "can liberate the world," as Palmer writes—enables the manager to fulfill an enobling mission to equip others to live lives that are productive and meaningful. Nothing less than this sense of holy purpose rooted in true inwardness—not widening profit margins or increased market share in and of itself—will provide institutional management with the interior sense of purpose and vision necessary for long-term leadership in an evolving and competitive world economy.

Biblically speaking, this life-orientation is an exercise in "kenotic" leadership. *Kenosis* is a Greek term used throughout the New Testament to denote "self-emptying." As we have seen, in Phillipians 2:7 Paul writes that Jesus "emptied himself [*kenosis*] and took on the role of a slave, being born in human likeness." For Christians, Jesus is the paradigm of the leader who divests himself of everything he has in order to serve others. By suspending his special standing as a member of the Godhead, Jesus kenotically performs leadership as service by becoming human and suffering death. He gives his life as a sacrifice so that all persons, indeed all of creation, would have the opportunity to experience new life. Nothing less is required of the contemporary leader, whether her sphere of influence be business, the academy, the professions, or religious ministries. If in fact the institutional leader truly envisions her task as a sacred trust nourished by a robust inner life, then she will risk everything—her professional reputation, her standing in the organization, her salary and pension—in order to move her colleagues and peers toward service of the greater good.

"When Jesus calls a person, he bids him 'come and die,'" said Dietrich Bonhoeffer.[15] His active resistance to the Nazis eventually led to his execution in the Flossenbürg concentration camp in 1945. Bonhoeffer's membership in the conspiracy reflected his reliance on his innermost discernment of the truth—what he called *conscience*—which guided him toward subverting the Third Reich in the early 1940s. He knew this was a risky proposition. On the one hand, he believed the government was from God and binding on conscience; deference to the governing authorities is the proper rule for citizens of the state.[16] On the other, he maintained that particular times of crisis might require a person to especially heed the voice of one's conscience—particularly under the tutelage of the Gospel message—and thereby take the risk of "bear[ing] guilt for the sake of charity."[17] In fidelity to conscience, one might find oneself running the risk of incurring guilt in pursuit of responsible action in service to the neighbor. At times, one must do what appears to be the wrong thing in order to pursue a higher good. Given his theology of the divine right of government, Bonhoeffer—in living out the dictates of his conscience and joining the conspiracy against Hitler—assumed the guilt of murder through disobeying the commandment of the Decalogue, "Thou shalt not kill."

Contemporary management theory says little about the practice of conscience or inner truth-seeking as the attitudinal disposition necessary for successful leadership. An exception is Peter Senge's *The Fifth Discipline*, which avoids the language of management formulas and techniques and focuses instead on the dimensions of character—specifically, commitment to truth, or conscience, in Bonhoeffer's vocabulary—as requisite for authentic leadership development:

> Commitment to the truth often seems to people an inadequate strategy. "What do I need to do to change my behavior?" "How do I change my underlying belief?" People often want a formula, a technique, something tangible that they can apply to solve the problem of structural conflict. But, in fact, being committed to the truth is far more powerful than any technique.

Commitment to the truth does not mean seeking the "Truth," the absolute final word or ultimate cause. Rather, it means a relentless willingness to root out the ways we limit or deceive ourselves from seeing what is, and to continually challenge our theories of why things are the way they are. . . . It also means continually deepening our understanding of the structures underlying current events.[18]

The kenotic leader has the courageous faith of Father Abraham who risked everything to follow God's command to sacrifice his son, what he knew to be the truth (so Genesis 22 for Jews and Christians, and Sura 32 in the Qu'ran for Muslims). The three Abrahamic traditions agree on this point: Abraham is a model of authentic leadership in our time because he followed the inner dictates of what he knew to be right even in the face of opposition and uncertainty. Nineteenth-century Danish philosopher Søren Kierkegaard analyzes the biblical account of Abraham's integrity as a follower of his own inward certainty. Abraham was a "knight of faith" who willingly took a "leap of faith" into the truth as he discerned it: "[The leap of faith] is the finest and the most extraordinary of all; it has an elevation of which I can certainly form a conception, but no more than that. I can make the mighty trampoline leap whereby I cross over into infinity. . . ."[19] No such leap would truly constitute a genuine vault into the void if the leader had all the information about the outcome of her leap at her immediate disposal. In fidelity to truth according to her own best lights, the leader takes a leap of faith where an "information gap," as Robert Greenleaf puts it, forces her to rely on "intuition" to bridge the abyss between what she does and does not know:

As a practical matter, on most important decisions there is an information gap. There usually is an information gap between the solid information in hand and what is needed. The art of leadership rests, in part, on the ability to bridge that gap by intuition, that is, a judgment from the unconscious process. The person who is better at this than most is likely to emerge as the leader because of the ability to contribute something of great value. Others will depend on such persons to go out ahead and show the way because their judgment will be better than most. Leaders, therefore, must be more creative than most; and creativity is largely discovery, a push into the uncharted and the unknown. Every once in a while a leader needs to think like a scientist, an artist, a poet. And a leader's thought processes may be just as fanciful as theirs—and as fallible.

Intuition is a *feel* for patterns, the ability to generalize based on what has happened previously. Wise leaders know when to bet on these intuitive leads, but they always know that they are betting on percentages. Their hunches are not seen as eternal truths.[20]

Barack Obama is an example of a leader who traded in his intuitional convictions and initiated his own leap of faith, in order to serve the greater good—and did so, potentially, at great cost to himself. In March 2008, Obama did what I thought was unheard of in the midst of a tightly wound presidential primary: he frankly and openly discussed the ugly racial divide that separates many Anglos from people of color in the United States.[21] Without rancor or bitterness, but fully acknowledging the pain and distress that racial prejudice foments in America,

Obama discussed such difficult topics as the problems with first-generation black liberation theology and the latent racist training within his own family of origin. I was stunned: here was a biracial, African American presidential candidate putting his political future on the line by opening, again, the great wound that continues to belie the promise of American exceptionalism—the wound of slavery, Jim Crow, and continuing institutional racism—the wound that will not heal. The contemporary leader committed to a larger purpose will similarly make herself vulnerable—she, too, will become a kenotic servant of others—in order to heal and unleash the buried liberatory energies within the wider community she cares for.

The journey *inward* toward one's vital life-source enables the self-emptying journey *outward* toward institutional leadership in organizations committed to genuine value. Perhaps few of us will be asked to give up our lives in the same manner that Jesus and Bonhoeffer did. But all of us are asked to become daily practitioners of self-emptying—to model to others how to put into abeyance attention to private interests in order to serve the well-being of the larger societies and ecosystems we inhabit. Kenotic service, however, is not *do-goodism, feel-good charity,* or *philanthropy* for its own sake. Indeed, it is not altruism as such. Rather, it is a passion for the health of the wider community, rooted in the inner certainties of the heart, that propels non-risk-averse organizations toward more humane and sustainable practices in the midst of competition, change, and uncertainty.

Successful leaders are everyday practitioners of the inner life who abandon a hierarchical model of controlling people and events in favor of a participatory model of engaging change with and for others in institutions that seek to be humanly just and environmentally sustainable. As William O'Brien, former C.E.O. of Hanover Insurance puts it, such persons shoulder "an almost sacred responsibility: to create conditions that enable people to have happy and productive lives."[22] The daily maintenance of one's vital life-source—obedience to conscience, truth, and the willingness to engage the unknown—is the wellspring that animates all authentically productive and transformative thought and action in the public sphere. Knowing full well the risks attendant upon such an inner journey, the leader kenotically forges ahead with a sense of certainty and mission about the sacred calling she fulfills by seeking the wellbeing of the wider social and ecological orders she serves.

Case Study of Landry's Bicycles

In this section I analyze Boston-based Landry's Bicycles' integrated focus on profit sharing and global mission as a case study of triple bottom line economics within a spiritual and moral worldview.[23] It is not an overstatement to say that Landry's Bicycles, founded in 1922, is in the business to save the world. This claim sounds grandiose. But having recently spent a couple of days with the company's owners, brothers Tom and Peter Henry, and conducting my own interviews and research, I believe that Landry's Bicycles is motivated by a visionary desire to better people's lives and to defend the planet through healthy, enjoyable cycling. Working between four stores and seventy-five employees, both men's sense of global mission is inextricably tied to their commitment to employee's well-being and the store's financial health. Landry's operates, in my judgment, with a missionary zeal to sell quality bikes at a reasonable price with an emphasis on customer service, equitable employee relations, and minimal impact on natural systems.

The company's core philosophy is best stated in its 2008 Buyer's Guide, "Bicycles are the Solution to Some of the World's Biggest Problems."[24] Landry's believes that, if it can persuade people to get out of their cars and onto bikes, then riders can save themselves from sedentary lifestyle diseases such as obesity and diabetes in developed countries like the U.S., and the planet will be protected from harmful tail-pipe emissions—the primary driver of human-induced global warming. Their motto is "Kick Gas."[25] For a bike dealership, is this catch phrase self-serving? Of course it is. But its point is that our fossil fuel economy is an addictive habit that keeps us hooked on a volatile resource that is expensive, unsustainable, and quickly disappearing. Our oil and fuel addiction is ruining our health, warping the economy, destroying the planet, and provoking international conflicts in oil rich countries (e.g., Iraq and the Caucasus). We need to move beyond carbon dependence, and using a bike helps to power down carbon-intensive lifestyles for the well-being of everyone, ourselves included.

In recent years, high levels of obesity and diabetes among adult and child populations have emerged as a community health epidemic in the developed world. Many Americans are becoming overweight and suffering from related diseases by relying on added high-fat and high-sugar diets. Landry's Bicycles is a beacon of light on a landscape pockmarked with poor nutrition and exercise habits. Its mission is to inculcate among consumers the habit of everyday cycling that challenges our increasingly deskbound culture of junk diets and indifference to physical health. Of course, owning a bike does not guarantee that a person's food choices and non-active life patterns will improve any more than membership in a health club ensures regular workout regimens for club members. But the store works hard to make cycling a fun and attractive option for persons of all ages and backgrounds. It treats every customer as an "honored guest" by making sure the cycling experience begins with a well-fitted bike tailored to the customer's body type and overall travel and recreation needs.[26] In theological terms, Landry's practices "hospitality to the stranger"—here we can think of Abraham's welcoming of the three visitors to his tent in Genesis 18—as basic to its core vision. Each individual shop has a fitting studio that integrates body and machine to enable riders to feel the power, control, and security that comes with a bike set up for him or her. When a person adds biking to their daily routine (or walking, running, or some other form of cardiovascular exercise) the move toward better personal health is subtle but profound. With a solid and comfortable bike at the ready, the potential increases for a systemic shift in one's daily routine that moves away from dependence on the automobile to a more grounded, active, nature-based, and enjoyable means of personal transportation.

Riding a bike can be basic to good fitness, but how does such activity generate "environmental capital"—increasing the value and health of the natural world—as well? Today's leadership challenge is to nurture successful "green" businesses that create financial, human, and natural capital through fair-minded management-employee programs and sustainable, low carbon emitting relations with the natural world. Landry's Bicycles shares this green vision: long-term profitability and customers' physical and spiritual well-being leader in a just and verdant world. How to realize this vision is essentially a *moral* question rather than a strictly business decision or narrow political issue. Smart and sustainable business practice is an ethical commitment to the wellbeing of the commons that cuts across competing economic models and partisan political lines.

Take the example of Arnold Schwarzenegger in this regard. Schwarzenegger, Republican governor of California, positions himself in the "conservative conservationist" tradition of Theodore Roosevelt, who spearheaded the modern parks system, and Richard Nixon, who founded the Environmental Protection Agency (EPA). He is opposed to drilling off the Pacific coast. He has offered large tax incentives to suppliers of alternative energy. Most controversially, he recently signed a bill to cut the state's greenhouse gas emissions for cars and trucks by 30% by 2015, along with a significant decrease of carbon content in transportation fuels. Until recently, Schwarzenegger was embroiled in a protracted battle with the previous administration of George W. Bush over the EPA's refusal to allow California (and twenty other states representing close to half of the nation's auto market) to implement strict tailpipe emissions standards because such standards would supposedly hurt the U.S. economy. The EPA sued California and California countersued the EPA; both cases are still pending.

California maintains that strong emissions guidelines will reposition the state as a world leader in developing greenhouse gas cutback technologies for cars and trucks. Conservation leadership, therefore, makes good business sense. The corporate world's single-minded focus on quarterly returns, according to Schwarzenegger, has blinded California, and the rest of the country, both to its long-term needs for energy independence and the importance of becoming a player in

the booming green jobs and green industry economies worldwide. Instead of relying on old polluting fossil fuel sources
to power California, the world's seventh largest economy,
Schwarzenegger wants his state to become a standard bearer
in renewable energy that promotes both financial and environmental prosperity for current and future residents.[27] I mention Schwarzenegger vis-à-vis Landry's to make the point that
Landry's, like the state of California, is trying to do its part
by incubating a long-term, triple bottom line business model
that addresses a central moral demand: creating economically
viable organizations that serve the social and environmental
needs of our time. This is an extremely difficult balancing
act to perform—and fair-minded people will disagree with
one another on how actually to make just and sustainable
institutions successful—but Landry's commitment to this
transformative business model distinguishes it as a leader in
corporate America.

Social Capital

A major test of an organization's social and environmental mission is the way in which it structures its common life together.
How an institution cares for its employees and staff, and the
manner in which it distributes resources and profits, reflects
its moral compass. Landry's takes seriously this aspect of its
mission. It has spearheaded a variety of revenue distributing
and profit sharing initiatives to stimulate economic growth and
create a better labor environment in the company. In part, its
goal is to generate what social scientists call "social capital"—
the added value of positive and productive interhuman relations. In this vein, consider the story of Landry's mechanic

José Ardon. José is a thirty-four year old immigrant from El Salvador who settled in the Boston area in 1995. At that time, he spoke marginal English and was not confident in his communication skills. He came to work at Landry's in 1996 as an entry level bike assembler and honed his craft, to the point that today he is one of the store's chief certified repair technicians as well as one of its "front shop" leaders. José both fixes bikes and directs the workflow through the store by greeting customers as they enter the store while he takes their repair orders. Similar to the Bangladeshi Grameen Bank microcredit program, José benefits from Landry's policy of redistributing to all mechanics 1 percent of labor revenue for the purchase of tools.[28] As is the case with almost all of Landry's mechanics, now he owns his own set of top quality Snap-On tools. Visiting with José in his workspace is like encountering a priest at the altar. Both venues are sacred space. José's work area is immaculately maintained and anchored by his gleaming red-and-white tool chest and bike repair mount. His tools are means of transformation (read: means of grace) as he puts together broken bikes and brings them back to life. And he does so with a buoyant attitude that radiates good feeling throughout the store. José's jubilatory craftsmanship completes the circle of Landry's employees relations philosophy: Landry's has helped to nurture José as a productive member of society who controls his own means of production and, in turn, José provides Landry's with an internally motivated, skilled professional who daily increases the company's value and worth.

When an employee develops her own sense of ownership about the obligations and mission of the company she works for—when she is motivated to seek the well-being of her home institution apart from external rewards and consequences—the

company discovers the "magic switch" that drives all successful enterprises. José is not a passive employee, who counts
the minutes until the end of the work day, but rather what
Tom Henry calls an active team member whose pride in his
work product is the foundation of Landry's governance structure. The company's revenue redistribution program is complemented by its profit sharing policy. The bulk of Landry's
profits (around 80 percent to 85 percent) are handed out to
employees with a smaller percentage (around 15 percent to 20
percent) ploughed back into the company's infrastructure and
inventory. This usually amounts to a $30,000.00 to $40,000.00
payout to employees along with a $5,000.00 to $8,000.00 return
to the company's reinvestment fund. In relation to their pay
grades, all salaried employees are annually rewarded a portion
of this extra tax-deferred income in order to build their retire-
ment accounts. This tax-deferred income is offered as a match
of employees' contributions to their 401k plans. Landry's pays
80 percent of individual medical plans (60 percent of family
plans). As well, it promotes a performance-based incentives
package for each store such that 5 percent of sales beyond
a twice-weekly sales goal—plus the difference between pay
budget and actual pay—goes back to employees. These various profit sharing and incentive programs create what Tom
Henry calls a "culture of recognition that celebrates achieve-
ment." These measures help to turn on the "magic switch" for
Landry's so that team members have a direct sense of ownership about the current mission and future progress of the
company. At its best, team members regard the company as a
stewardship held in common trust, a workplace where people
as people are valued, even loved.[29] Tom Henry writes about
his organizational philosophy in this regard:

Seen as a whole, an organization is a living, breathing, feeling, thinking being—as capable of love and being loved an any individual person. When looked at as a living being, an organization can seem to be looking back at us as if it had a consciousness of its own. We are not masters of the organization. At best, we are stewards. Love (as a pure desire for wholeness, in oneself, in others, in the world) is the great theme of [our model]. Love is the underlying mystery of [a sound organizational] model. Care for the growth of the people within our organization, desire to serve the common good of our world, and stewardship of our power and money as means to good ends—these are the variations on the theme of love in [this] model.[30]

Landry's financial model is a *mixed economy*. It is a capitalist enterprise insofar as the means of production are owned by two individuals (Tom and Peter Henry); it operates in a relatively open, free market environment that stimulates innovation and entrepreneurial risk taking; and its goal is to develop and sustain long-term business viability for its employees and investors. These three "capitalist" factors—private ownership, free markets, and profit-making—are balanced, however, by the company's "socialist" commitments to collective profit sharing. In particular, the company rejects *laissez-faire*, Milton Friedman-style capitalism: the argument that maximizing profits at all costs is the "business of business" that trumps all other values. It champions social and environmental responsibility *as well as* long-term financial stability. Tom Henry writes:

In everything we do at Landry's, we are committed to *making the world a better place.* We respect the communities we live and work in, we care for our natural and built environments, and we watch over them for the benefit of future generations . . . [and] we care for our operations to ensure Landry's *long-term business viability* for the mutual benefit of our employees, customers, suppliers, and investors. Profitability isn't the only thing, but it's nevertheless a critical measure of our shared success.[31]

Landry's capitalist/socialist dialectic is a move beyond the company's more egalitarian pay scale initiated in the 1980s. At that time it experimented with a flat pay scale in which all employees, owners included, received the same compensation. But Tom and Peter decided this model sapped the company of the entrepreneurial spirit that is now being generated by a structured, incentives-based pay arrangement. Tom says this recent innovation is not set in stone. But the question of compensation is an important issue for the company that bears on its long-term financial viability. The current ownership group hopes to restructure ownership of the company by eventually transferring control of the store to a new group of "in-house" investors—what Tom calls "workers-owners"—with the same drive and vision that the Henrys have sought to embody. Their goal is not to bleed the company of its assets, line their own pockets, and then leave, but rather to preserve the company's *value*—in every sense of that term—and then hand over the stewardship of Landry's to a new generation of "workers-owners." How to ensure its essential culture and mission—how to balance its well publicized attention to ecoresponsibility ("Kick Gas") and social values (store management as "worker-owners") along with its focus on the financial bottom line in both short and long terms—is an extraordinary challenge Landry's Bicycles now faces in earnest.

Challenges to the Model

Landry's is a compelling case study of triple bottom-line thinking. It has worked hard to model fair-minded governance and compensation practices with its staff, preserve its long-term business viability through a focus on its global mission, and, it is not too grandiose to say, save the planet through cycling. Among its other civic outreach efforts, Landry's is a leader in the Bikes Belong coalition that works with local and national governments to promote public health and happiness through projects that encourage bicycling.[32] But has Landry's gone far enough in confronting the challenge of doing business in a world tilting toward environmental collapse? Has Landry's systemically incorporated sustainability values in *all* of its operations, or has it, rather, made a half turn to green practices, not a full turn? Is the company essentially not a revolutionary but a reformist organization that promotes a more socially just and sustainable *form* of capitalism—capitalism with a human face, as it were—but not a radical *challenge* to the economic status quo as such?

Whether Landry's business model is adequate to the global crisis is a question I will not fully answer here. An answer to this question, however, will reflect the revolutionary versus the reformist approaches in contemporary sustainable business theory. From the revolutionary perspective, capitalism, by definition, is woefully unable to stop harm to workers and planetary destruction because it is a morally indifferent, market-driven enterprise. Markets are profit-oriented. Today's markets are highly sophisticated at delivering goods and services at prices that maximize shareholders' *wealth*, but they are not good at *ethically* measuring the true impact on workers and the environment of the goods and services they produce. Markets are designed to maximize owners' profits, not engage in full-cost accounting. As Paul Hawken argues, the forces that drive markets toward greater profitability for shareholders are diametrically opposed to the well-being of workers and the environment:

> Businesses do not need to recognize sustainability in order to succeed. They don't have to take into account that their present demands on resources are tantamount to stealing from the future, or that selling today's wants is at the expense of tomorrow's needs. Nor does business have to acknowledge the devastating legacy of toxins and waste it is passing off to future generations. In fact, businesses are usually "better off" ignorant of these facts and principles if they intend to prosper in the present economic system . . . Thus, the commercial acts that would lead us away from runaway ecological devastation, although sound in the principles of nature, are unsound by the standards of the economy.[33]

Hawken and others call for a "restorative economy" that will "end industrialism as we know it."[34] For these critics, capitalist economics is akin to the old Soviet system that was ideologically wedded to large-scale trampling of workers' rights and destruction of the planet for short-term rewards. Only a revolutionary response to the current crisis—only a full-scale governmental intervention into market capitalism that balances the needs of labor and the environment over and against shareholders' interests—can remake Western civilization so that it is no longer at war with its mass of human inhabitants and the wider Earth itself.

Savitz takes issue with Hawken by shifting the focus away from capitalism's inherent unresponsiveness to the current crisis to the flexible entrepreneurial energy within many companies to promote fair labor and conservation practices. In the long run (and here we need only reference the U.S. auto industry as exhibit A), corporations must become self-consciously sustainable—in both economic *and* environmental terms—or they will lose market share and eventually die. Savitz would agree with Hawken that capitalism's mantra is "the business of business is business," but he would emphasize, in reformist rather than revolutionary terms, that the profit motive *itself* is propelling many institutions toward better labor relations and sustainability efforts because such moves improve the company's bottom line. Sustainability, in short, is good business. Even without direct government regulatory efforts,

> countless corporations have voluntarily improved their environmental performance for financial reasons . . . many companies have also found ways to invest in workers, consumers, or the community that provide excellent financial returns. So even in a world of short-term profit maximizers, companies may behave responsibly, and often do.
>
> The cynics say that these changes have come at the margins, that they have not gone nearly far enough to save the world. This is true, but we see reason to be

hopeful in the fact that business leaders are now realizing that many more forms of corporate responsibility
can help maximize profits and minimize risk in the long
run. And as that idea takes hold, more dramatic, positive
changes are in store.[35]

Earlier I noted how the Seeing Things Whole organization enables companies to reconceive their mission in broader
social terms. Seeing Things Whole has consulted with Landry's
Bicycles in order to create an overarching perspective on institutional performance that opens up opportunities for genuine
conversation and self-criticism from a variety of stakeholders
in the company's future. It has helped Landry's to better articulate its purpose, with its struggles and its promise held in tension. By my count, Landry's has submitted itself to more than
a dozen evaluation and critique sessions sponsored by Seeing
Things Whole in which Landry's management team has continued to revise and strengthen its responsibilities to employees' well-being and care of creation. Reflecting back on this
process, Benefiel and Hamilton write:

> In the case of SeeingThingsWhole and Landry's Bicycles,
> the spiritual roots of both organizations were woven into
> an action-oriented process. Through reflection and con-
> templation, this has created an ongoing transformation
> for Landry's Bicycles for over a decade. . . . This method
> created change in both a senior executive and an execu-
> tive team that served to strengthen the company culture.
> Ultimately, the intervention has created a positive sus-
> tained change of family spirit and love in this company.
> In both cases, cooperative inquiry engaged employees,
> resulted in positive organizational change, and created

knowledge that could be used by the companies in the future.[36]

Whether capitalism needs systemic overall (Hawken) or reformation from within (Savitz) in order to become sustainable is an important question that can be approached but not fully answered here. But whether Landry's triple bottom line model has fully coordinated its financial, social, and ecological interests is a question best answered by attending to the painstaking self-evaluation process that animates Landry's culture—a mixed economic culture that seeks to realize profitability and sustainability as flip sides of the same coin.

In spite of the debate by some about the causes of climate change, climatologists agree that the prospects for human well-being on Earth are bleak. In reply, to borrow Thomas Berry's phrase, every generation has its "great work."[37] In this generation, our ennobling work will be to fight environmental degradation by reimagining our relationship to living things as fellow and sister travelers on a fragile planet—a planet that cries out for nurture and compassion, not exploitation and abuse. This is the sustainability mandate of our time. But will we be able to seize this moment and nurture new modes of existence so that this and future generations can live richer and more productive lives? A first step will be to wean ourselves off unsustainable coal, oil, and natural gas supplies in order to save the planet. A second will be to imagine and build viable institutions that are financially sound, protective of the natural world, and enriching and meaningful for families and wage earners alike.

This chapter maintains that a business committed to sustainable living and its corresponding health benefits realizes the biblical ideal of loving one's body buoyed by a healthy, verdant natural world. Like the previous chapter's analysis of a fresh foods store as a case study of green Christianity in action, this chapter makes a similar point: businesses like Landry's Bikes that grow natural, social and economic capital are the living institutional reality of this book's theological ideal of practicing Christianity with an emancipatory intent.

We need businesses and institutions that live by economically and environmentally sustainable ideals that coordinate the values of social capital, financial stability, and planetary health. I know from working with college students that most young people want to live for something greater than themselves, to align their lives with a sacred purpose that gives meaning to their daily commitments and obligations. With the current economic downturn, it appears the wheels of history have turned again: the era of unfettered capitalism is over and the time has passed when maximizing shareholder profits as the supreme good is all that matters. Today's sustainable businesses look instead to a higher calling: to produce and market goods and services that include the interests of *all* stakeholders—and not just corporate shareholders—for the good of human flourishing and the welfare of the biosphere. This is Christianity in our time. This is the challenge of our generation. This is our sacred mission. The triple bottom line model can help us to achieve this goal, and, with this ideal as our lodestar, we will be empowered to seek and enhance genuine institutional viability, the public good, and the welfare of our planet home.

Chapter Six

CASE STUDIES
OF SPIRITUAL
ECOLOGY

"Whatever your values are, you have to practice
them, they have to be embodied in daily activity."
Clare Butterfield, "Food for Faith," Renewal

RENEWAL

Not just Christianity but *all* of the world's religions are a
trove of ideas and practices for cultivating green, body-loving
habits of heart and mind. This chapter expands the horizon
of concern for planetary and bodily well-being beyond the
Christian message to include the harvest of global spiritual
resources that offers all of us grounds for hope. This harvest
is wide and bountiful, and it is available not only through
sacred books and contemporary writings but also through
another medium that is visually and viscerally immediate:

documentary film. The wager of this chapter is that viewing the *Renewal* DVD that accompanies this book will tap the rich vein of people and actions that make up the religious environmental movement today, inspiring readers to join with others' or develop their own practices of Earth solidarity and love of one's flesh.

Renewal is a feature-length documentary that offers viewers eight compelling stories of religious-environmental activism. The stories range from Christian protests against mountaintop removal coal mining in Appalachia, to Chicago Muslims partnering with rural farmers to produce organic meat products, to Jewish children in Connecticut learning how to practice Earth-based religion founded on the time-honored beliefs of their ancestors. Filmmakers Marty Ostrow and Terry Kay Rockefeller bring to life the stories of everyday prophets, poets, and preachers who are doing their part to green the planet and care for the physical well-being of the communities and congregations they serve. This chapter can be used for individual reader's edification and for larger church and neighborhood groups who want a variety of resources for getting started with green living from a spiritual perspective. For each of the eight stories I provide a narrative summary, pose questions viewers can ask themselves, and present information about print, Internet, and other media resources for learning about the emerging religious-environmental movement. Like other mass liberation movements in Western history— civil rights, German reunification, Anglo-Irish peace talks—this movement is fueled by the foresight and energy of spiritual visionaries who use the power of religious symbols and rhetoric to promote change.

1. A Crime against Creation

Narrative

In the opening episode of *Renewal*, we watch an ecumenical gathering of witness and resistance to the practice of mountaintop removal in the hills of Appalachia in Eastern Kentucky. Christians of different denominations travel to Appalachia on a listening tour to learn about how large mountainous areas are destroyed in order to extract seams of coal. The story is a heartfelt cry for environmental justice for all populations of living things: animals, plants, and human beings. For the religious leaders on this tour, the destruction of God's creation also entails the undermining of human health. Whenever natural resources are extracted without attention to their negative health effects, the "garden of the Lord," as the episode's haunting opening song puts it, is laid to waste, and all of God's creatures, including the human community, are degraded in the process.

To me, the most moving moment in this episode is when the mother of a little girl narrates what is happening to her daughter when she bathes in water now made toxic from the coal recovery process. "We have well water that is contaminated," says the mother. "It has high levels of arsenic in it. My child bathes in this water and tries to drink the bubbles in the water. She doesn't understand this is going to hurt her, she is just three years old." The viewer is left with a sick feeling in her stomach after watching this exchange. Has our culture descended to the point at which we trade the well-being of our children for generating revenue through fossil fuels exploitation?

Other scenes from the episode sear the viewer's imagination as she witnesses what happens when whole mountains are blown away to extract coal: the rumble of dynamite in the background, the grey clouds of coal dust wafting dark and menacing on the horizon, the outstretched arms of the traveling Christians now gathered as a community of worship on the plateau of a newly split-open mountaintop. The episode ends with a call to commitment by Peter Illyn of "Restoring Eden": Will those assembled on the mountaintop—and, by implication, we the viewers of this episode—renounce our addiction to unsustainable fossil fuels? Can we envision a new moral and economic order in which planetary waste is no longer a prerequisite for human habitation?

Questions

1. What is the nature of sin in an age of ecological peril? This episode reintroduces the language of sin, an uncomfortable topic for many persons, religious or otherwise. Sin here is not understood in terms of discrete acts of commission but as our unrecognized complicity with systems of structural oppression that destroy life as we know it. The vignette about the three-year-old drinking arsenic-laced bubbles in her bath water makes this point with biting clarity. Are we not commiting the sin of infanticide by sacrificing our children to maintaining the false idol of the American Way of Life? Have we lost our way—in religious terms, have we sold our souls—to the counterfeit god of money and wealth? Whom do we really worship, the Creator of the biblical witness, or the toxic divinities of Big Coal and Big Oil? No Christian

today—no person of conscience and good faith—would consider owning a human slave. At one time, however, many American Christians considered slavery a divinely mandated institution. Will the day come when people of faith regard nonsustainable energy use—buying cheap power, driving an SUV—as a sin against God, a crime against creation, as the title of this episode puts it?

2. A second question emerges here, namely: Is religion necessary for saving the planet? Implicitly, this episode makes the claim that without a conversion of the heart to Earth-centered living no long-term commitment to environmental sustainability is viable. The world's religions seek to involve the whole person in movements of personal and social transformation. If this is the case, does religious belief and practice provide the necessary foundation for genuine and lasting sustainable social policy? In the case of Appalachia, is knowledge about mountaintop removal enough to stop the destruction? Or do communities of resistance need the symbolic resources of religious faith to propel them over the long haul to stop the degradation of what is for them the good creation God has made? In other words, is the environmental crisis we now face—figured so graphically in this episode about Eastern Kentucky—essentially not a problem of the head (not a problem concerning what we do and do not know about the crisis and its causes) but a problem of the heart (a problem that requires out whole personhood to become committed to sustainable existence as a way of life)? If this is the case, then is religion—as one of, if not the most potent motivators of the human heart—fundamentally necessary for

engendering and sustaining our collective efforts to preserve creation?

Resources

"Can Religion Save the Environment?" *E: The Environmental
    Magazine* 13, November/December 2002.
Evangelical Environmental Network. www.esa-online.org/een
McFague, Sallie. *A New Climate for Theology: God, the World,
    and Global Warming.* Minneapolis: Fortress, 2008.
Gebara, Ivone. *Longing for Running Water: Ecofeminism and
    Liberation.* Minneapolis: Fortress, 1999.
Grey, Mary. *Sacred Longings: The Ecological Spirit and Global
    Culture.* Minneapolis: Fortress, 2004.
Is God Green? Directed by Bill Moyers. Arlington, Va.: Public
    Broadcasting Service, 1996. Also available online at: http://
    www.pbs.org/moyers/moyersonamerica/green/watch.
    html.
Wallace, Mark I. *Finding God in the Singing River: Christian-
    ity, Spirit, Nature.* Minneapolis: Fortress, 2005.

2. Going Green

Narrative

The message of this episode is that American churches are
beginning to take seriously a new mandate to save the Earth
by changing their concrete institutional practices. This episode
narrates the story of "Green Faith," an interfaith environmental
coalition in New Jersey that empowers religious congregations
to install solar panels without any up-front cost on the part

of the congregation. Solar panels take clean energy from the sun and then convert it into electrical power. This new technology enables many institutions, such as churches, to buy less gas and coal-derived energy—and thereby do their part to save the planet from global warming, which in large part is driven by heat-trapping fossil fuel burning and emissions. Here we see the Revs. Stephanie and Seth Kaper-Dale of the Reformed Church of Highland Park organize the installation of a solar panel array on the roof of their church. The scenes of the bright shiny panels atop the Highland Park church make a bold statement to potential members about the relevance of local congregations to blunting the impact of climate change through their institutional choices. As Seth Kaper-Dale puts it, "The thing that brought these [new members] into the congregation was seeing solar panels on the roof of the church."

Now twenty-four New Jersey places of worship have solar panel installations; and other Earth-keeping programs have been similarly started, such as trash assessments that lead to new congregational recycling programs. This episode focuses on one such waste audit ritual at the Highland church. After the pastors and church members examine the trash generated during a typical week at the church, they develop practical strategies for reducing their contribution to the waste stream: using mugs instead of styrofoam cups, setting up clearly marked bins for recyclable materials, and establishing a new composting regimen instead of throwing out their organic waste. Church members then gather in a prayer circle to sing hymns and celebrate their new-found commitment to healing creation. I found this green liturgy to be especially meaningful. After the pastors recount how many barrels of oil and pounds of coal have been saved by converting to solar energy, members of the circle exclaim responsorially, "Thanks be to God." Going green and worshipping God are now viewed as one and the same reality.

Questions

1. In this story, the Rev. Fletcher Harper of Green Faith says, "These big black panels on churches make the statement that here is a house of worship that believes deeply in protecting the Earth." This comment raises, therefore, an important question: What specific initiatives can religious congregations and related institutions, such as seminaries and universities, take to begin their own commitment to saving the planet from global warming? Should the installation of solar panels—or some other form of energy co-production—now be regarded as necessary by all faith-based communities and organizations committed to wise Earth stewardship? Places of worship and centers of higher learning are, in many respects, leading the institutional charge against climate change. They are developing alternative energy sources for their own physical plants, converting their transportation fleets to hybrid and other high mileage vehicles, and sourcing their food and other consumables such as paper and coffee through sustainable and often local vendors. What concrete steps should religious and educational organizations take to address an increasingly warming planet in our time?

2. This episode narrates a trash audit ritual in which congregational members inventory the impact of their discarded items on the waste stream and then commit

liturgically to changing their wasteful habits. Creation-based liturgy is an exciting new development within contemporary churches, synagogues, mosques, and temples. Ecoliturgy enables long-term commitments to environmental wellbeing by touching congregants on the level of their deepest emotions to care about and thereby heal the Earth. What role, therefore, should "green" liturgy and homiletics now play in the common worship and institutional life of American Christians and other people of faith? What fresh and dynamic symbols, imagery, hymns, prayers, litanies, confessions and blessings are being employed—or could be imagined—as central resources for today's emerging worshipping communities committed to Earth healing? What are the prospects, and the potential pitfalls, of such innovations as leading edge congregations develop new rites of healing and reconnecting with the Earth?

Resources

Association for the Advancement of Sustainability in Higher Education. www.aashe.org.

Creighton, Sarah Hammond. *Greening the Ivory Tower: Improving the Environmental Track Record of Universities, Colleges, and Other Institutions.* Cambridge: M.I.T. Press, 1998.

Gottlieb, Roger S., ed., *The Oxford Handbook of Religion and Ecology* (New York: Oxford University Press, 2006).

Green Faith. www.greenfaith.org.

Habel, Norman C. *Seven Songs of Creation: Liturgies for Celebrating and Healing Earth.* Cleveland: Pilgrim, 2004.

Kearns, Laurel, and Catherine Keller, eds. *Eco-Spirit: Religions and Philosophies for the Earth*. New York: Fordham University Press, 2007.

Moore, Mary Elizabeth. *Ministering with the Earth*. St. Louis: Chalice, 1998.

Rhoads, David, ed. *Earth and Word: Classic Sermons on Saving the Planet*. New York: Continuum, 2007.

The Green Bible: New Revised Standard Version. San Francisco: HarperOne, 2008.

3. Food for Faith

Narrative

This episode opens with a luminous sunrise over farmers' fields in southern Illinois and a hauntingly beautiful call to prayer from the Northbrook Mosque in suburban Chicago. This strange juxtaposition of rural landscape and urban Islam sets the tone for the story. It narrates how Shireen Pishdadi and other members of the Northbrook congregation; the Rev. Clare Butterfield of Faith in Place, a Christian interfaith environmental organization; and local organic farmers, such as Floyd Johnson, have partnered together to provide the Chicago Muslim community with farm-fresh meat that is humanely raised and meets Islamic dietary requirements (or *zabiha* in Arabic). This farm-to-city program is called *taqwa*, a Qur'anic term that means the practice of daily piety in all aspects of one's life. In this episode, *taqwa* stands for the refusal of Chicago Muslims to eat factory-processed meat products where, for example, chickens are kept in battery cages, their beaks and toes are cut off, and they are pumped full of antibiotics to prevent disease caused by over-crowded conditions. *Taqwa* offers an alternative by connecting ethically aware consumers to sustainable farmers around the habit of good eating.

As Ms. Pishdadi says, "The whole [farm-to-city] experience has really changed my life because I never questioned the food I ate, [but] the prophet Mohammed taught us to be kind to animals, to treat them with respect and dignity." Clare Butterfield helped to bring together Shireen Pishdadi's fellow congregants, who were looking for alternatives to cruelly raised and chemically saturated meat products, and farmers like Floyd Johnson, who wanted a market for their organic foods. But the suspicion that many Americans harbor toward Muslims after the events of 9/11 gave Johnson an initial pause. "At first I hesitated [to partner with the Muslims] because you hear about the Muslims and the terrorists, but I've enjoyed meeting Shireen and getting to know her and her ways." Local, sustainable eating is an ethical response to the Abrahamic religions' command to care for creation, and it heals the ugly divide that separates the People of the Book from one another.

"Muslims frown upon people eating alone," says Pishdadi. "The more people eat together, the more blessings are in the food." The episode ends with a call to prayer and a communal interfaith meal between Muslims, Christians, and others, where the food served and the fellowship enjoyed models the "way the world should be—this feeds us as much as the organic meat," as the Rev. Butterfield puts it.

Questions

1. "The food itself is a prayer," says Butterfield in this story. This comment raises an important question, namely:

What moral obligations do people of faith owe to the
animal world? Many of the world's religions prohibit the
inhumane treatment of animals, but none of the religions (with the exception of historic clerical Buddhism)
contain outright bans against eating meat. In response,
one might note the evolution in the Bible from a veg-
etarian to a non-vegetarian ideal. In Genesis 1:29-30,
Adam and Eve are given all green things as good to eat;
but in Genesis 9:3, God says, "Every moving thing that
lives shall be food for you; and [just] as I gave you the
green plants, I give you everything." The biblical shift
from plant foods to animal flesh consumption marks an
important change in divinely sanctioned food practices.
So the question is: Is eating meat morally and religiously
defensible? If not, why not? And if so, under what conditions and for what purpose?

2. After 9/11, graffiti appeared in many American cities
that read "Religion Kills." But this episode shows how
Muslims and Christians can come together around like-
minded partnerships that stress sustainable farming and
ethical eating. Common service projects, interfaith scriptural study, and now integrated food consumption work
are candidates for forging links between Muslims and
Christians in an era marked by the so-called global war
on terror. As Butterfield puts it, her work is based on
"the religious idea that whatever your values are, you
have to practice them, that they have to be embodied
in daily activity." *Apropos* this segment, what interfaith
efforts (environmental or otherwise) have you seen
work—or can you imagine—that bring together, rather
than divide, Muslims and Christians today?

Resources

Animals, Nature, and Religion. Directed by the Center for Respect of Life and Environment. Rockville, Md.: Video on Location, 1988.

Foltz, Richard C., and Frederick M. Denny, eds., *Islam and Ecology: A Bestowed Trust.* Cambridge, Mass.: Harvard University Press, 2003.

Islamic Foundation for Ecology and Environmental Sciences. www.unep.org/ourplanet/imgversn/82/khalid.html.

Light, Andrew, and Holmes Rolston III, eds. *Environmental Ethics: An Anthology.* Malden, Mass.: Blackwell, 2003.

Nasr, Seyyed Hossein. "Islam and the Environmental Crisis." In *Spirit and Nature: Why the Environment Is a Religious Issue,* edited by Stephen C. Rockefeller and John C. Elder, 85-107. Boston: Beacon, 1992.

National Religious Partnership for the Environment. www.nrpe.org.

Singer, Peter. *Animal Liberation.* New York: HarperCollins, 1975, 2002.

Waldau, Paul, and Kimberley Patton, eds. *A Communion of Subjects: Animals in Religion, Science, and Ethics.* New York: Columbia University Press, 2006.

4. Ancient Roots

Narrative

This episode begins with a joyous and rambunctious opening to a Jewish environmental camp for kids at the Teva Learning Center in Falls Village, Connecticut (*teva* is the Hebrew word for nature). Richard Louv's *Last Child in the Woods: Saving*

Our Children from Nature-Deficit Disorder argues that the core environmental literacy that pre-information age children used to enjoy has been lost on the current generation of sedentary kids, who seem addicted to digital media and rarely go outdoors. In this episode, as the campers prepare for a day in the woods at Teva, one girl, when asked if she ever plays outside, replies, "We have parks but we don't go into the trees or anything [because] we keep to the walking [paths]." At Teva, campers go into the woods. Under the leadership of Nili Simhai, the camp's curriculum is planned around the "central issue for our generation, Where are we going as a human community on this planet?"

Teva campers learn about photosynthesis, soil composition, care of farm animals, and organic farming. They also learn about how not to waste food. Rabbi Fred Scherlinder-Dobb of Adat Shalom Reconstructionist Synagogue says that Judaism's 530th commandment (out of a total of 613) is "do not waste" (or *bal tashit* in Hebrew). After eating, the kids at Teva scrape their leftover food into a waste bucket, weigh it, and then enter into a group competition with themselves to see whether they can reduce their food waste (by week's end, they are successful). The episode ends with a visit to Adamah, a Jewish organic farm (adjacent to Teva) for college-age students and young adults, which teaches how the whole person, not just the natural world, is renewed when healthy land practices are developed. Here Judaism exists outside the book and the synagogue in the green land that flows with the planting and reaping rhythms of ancient Judaism. Scenes of young people harvesting kale, sowing seeds, eating just-picked, sun-ripened watermelon—all in an attitude of blessing and gratitude—are beautifully choreographed in this episode.

Adamah brings together environmental renewal and the formation of leaders within American Judaism. Together, Teva and Adamah auger well for a new Jewish youth movement, a new green Judaism.

Questions

    1. As in the previous episode, "Food for Faith," one of the values of religious environmentalism here is to reconnect farmers and urban dwellers. How do we get our food? Where does it come from? What can we do to encourage sustainable and organic farming? As individuals and members of larger communities, what can we do to promote local sustainable agriculture? Many families and individuals today rely on Community Supported Agriculture (CSA) to source their weekly needs for fresh produce and other farm-raised foodstuffs, such as meat and dairy. Farmers sell their product at a set price to a guaranteed consumer market, and in turn the consumer experiences the wonder of local, organic produce outside the confines of the industrial agriculture complex. Institutions are just beginning to catch the CSA fever as well. What role could worshipping communities play in supporting and being supported by the emerging CSA movement?

    2. Teva and Adamah promote human well-being in a verdant world. The underlying thesis of this and all the stories in *Renewal* is that the environmental crisis, at its core, is less a scientific or technological problem and more a spiritual problem because it is human beings' deep ecocidal dispositions toward nature that are the cause of the

Earth's continued degradation. The crisis, as I said earlier, is a matter of the heart, not the head. Regarding the environmental crisis as a spiritual crisis, this episode seeks to recover the biocentric convictions within Jewish belief and practice as valuable resources for countering the exploitative and utilitarian attitudes toward Earth community that now dominate the global economic marketplace. In this episode, for example, Rabbi Scherlinder-Dobb alludes to the pun in the Book of Genesis regarding the human person (*adam*) and the Earth (*adamah*), which signals that humans are best understood as "Earth creatures" or "earthlings." What other biblical and rabbinic resources within Judaism also support this ideal? Similarly, in Christianity and Islam as well?

Resources

Bernstein, Ellen. *The Splendor of Creation: A Biblical Ecology.* Cleveland: Pilgrim, 2005.

Coalition on the Environment and Jewish Life. www.coejl.org

Elon, Ari, et al., eds. *Trees, Earth, and Torah: A Tu B'Shvat Anthology.* Philadelphia: Jewish Publication Society, 1999.

Gottlieb, Robert S. *A Greener Faith: Religious Environmentalism and Our Planet's Future.* Oxford: Oxford University Press, 2006.

Green, Arthur. "God, World, Person: A Jewish Theology of Creation, Parts I and II." *The Melton Journal* 24/25 (Spring 1991/92): 4-7, 4-5.

Louv, Richard. *Last Child in the Woods: Saving Our Children from Nature-Deficit Disorder.* Chapel Hill, N.C.: Algonquin Books, 2005.

Tirosh-Samuelson, Hava, ed. *Judaism and Ecology: Created World and Revealed Word.* Cambridge: Harvard University Press, 2003.

Waskow, Arthur. *Down-to-Earth Judaism: Food, Money, Sex, and the Rest of Life.* New York: Quill, William Morrow, 1995.

Zuckerman, Seth. "Redwood Rabbis." In *This Sacred Earth: Religion, Nature, Environment,* edited by Roger S. Gottlieb. 2nd edition, 644-50. New York: Routledge, 2004.

5. Compassion in Action

Narrative

This story begins with Lauren Van Ham's recounting of the tree ordination movement in modern Thailand. Buddhist monks wrapped trees targeted for logging with saffron-colored monastic robes; by "ordaining" the threatened trees, the monks convinced loggers, amazingly, to refuse to cut large swaths of virgin forests still remaining after generations of unsustainable timber extraction practices. Van Ham and other members of her "Green Sangha" Buddhist eco-community in San Francisco, use this story as justification of a sustained campaign to persuade environmentally aware magazines such as *National Geographic* and *The New Yorker* to switch to post-consumer, recycled paper products. Her "spiritually based environmental activism," as she puts it, uses letter-writing and petition-signing to persuade outsized multinational corporations to go green.

The episode focuses on the practice of sitting meditation within Green Sangha as the living ground of compassionate environmental engagement. Sitting meditation—called *zazen* in Japanese Zen Buddhism—enables spiritual activists to overcome frustration and anger by placing the devotee in a clear and open space. In this positive space of non-action, ironically, genuinely productive action is nurtured and sustained. As Buddhist practitioner Jonathan Gustin says, the key insight that undergirds this practice is the Buddhist teaching about the fundamental *non-separation* between human beings and all other forms of being (including water, soil, air and the myriads of non-human creatures who live on Earth). Nothing is independent of anything else because all things—human and nonhuman, sentient and nonsentient—are "empty" as co-participants in the ever-changing "flux" of reality. Ethically and politically speaking, non-separation means that large corporate entities like magazine publishers are potential allies, and never enemies, in the struggle to promote sustainable production and consumption. "When you act from non-separation," says Gustin, "you always make friends." This non-separation worldview—now daily enacted through contemplative practice—empowers a green activism that is both environmentally sustainable and emotionally fulfilling. This type of activism comes from a place of loving, mindful engagement with the needs and concerns of others. In green Buddhism, we are not ideological opponents struggling over dwindling resources but interconnected brothers and sisters on an evolving planet who mutually depend upon one another for life and wellbeing.

Questions

1. This story makes the case for Buddhist ethical practice. But does Buddhism have an environmental ethic? How

can a tradition that valorizes emptiness and flux engender a positive environmental ethic? Today, green Buddhists seek to correlate historical Buddhism (that is, the teachings of the Buddha) with current Earth-friendly understandings of Buddhism by using terms and phrases such as *compassion, nonviolence, middle path, Buddhahood of all things*, and the *interrelational self.* Can the time-honored non-Western beliefs and practices of Buddhism be translated into an American idiom that makes sense in the face of the ecocrisis? And if so, how might this new (but still ancient) "Eastern" vocabulary challenge and reshape the largely biblical worldview of much of North America?

2. This story also makes a case for meditation as the basis of environmental activism. Might the introduction of this activity to the wider environmental movement be one of the signal practices religious persons bring to make ecological activism more balanced and holistic? The argument here is that lobbying for change and other forms of direct-action politicking are not enough; quiet, contemplative work is also needed to supplement the high-octane public struggle to save the planet. In religious terms, no form of activism, environmental or otherwise, is sustainable over the long haul unless it comes from a place of mindfulness within each individual person. The goal of green Buddhism is to coordinate the inner landscape of the heart—care of oneself—with the outer landscape of Earth-caring for creation. Soulcraft and ecoactivism are flip sides of the same coin. Is this double attention to self-honoring meditation and Earth-honoring action, therefore, a particularly important

contribution by the religious community to the environmental movement today?

Resources

Batchelor, Martine, and Kerry Brown, eds., *Buddhism and Ecology*. London: Cassell, 1992.

Cook, Francis. "The Jewel Net of Indra." In *Nature in Asian Traditions of Thought: Essays in Environmental Philoso-phy,* edited by J. Baird Callicott and Roger T. Ames, 213-29. Albany, N.Y.: SUNY, 1989.

Dalai Lama. foreword to *Dharma Gaia: A Harvest of Essays in Buddhism and Ecology*. Edited by Allan Hunt Badiner. Berkeley, Calif.: Parallax, 1990.

Earth Sangha. www.earthsangha.com.

Kaza, Stephanie, and Kenneth Kraft, eds. *Dharma Rain: Sources of Buddhist Environmentalism*. Boston: Shamb-hala Publications, 2000.

McDaniel, Jay B. "Revisioning God and the Self: Lessons from Buddhism." In *Liberating Life: Contemporary Approaches to Ecological Theology,* edited by Charles Birch, William Eakin, and Jay B. McDaniel, 228-57. Maryknoll, N.Y.: Orbis, 1990.

Nhat Hanh, Thich. *Love in Action: Writings on Nonviolent Social Change*. Berkeley, Calif.: Parallax, 1993.

Sandell, Klas, ed., *Buddhist Perspectives on the Ecocrisis*. Kandy, Sri Lanka: Buddhist Publication Society, 1987.

Swearer, Donald K. *The Buddhist World of Southeast Asia*. Albany, N.Y.: SUNY, 1995; rev. ed., Chiang Mai, Thailand: Silkworm Books, 2007.

Tricycle Magazine. www.tricylce.com

6. Eco-Justice

Narrative

The plight of poor communities living in close proximity to hazardous industrial and waste-treatment industries is highlighted here. Moss Point and Escatawpa, Mississippi, are blighted coastal towns precariously located next to large oil-refining and gas-processing plants in nearby Pascagoula. Like Moss Point and Escatawpa, many residential populations existing next to polluting industries suffer from disproportionate toxic contamination problems, including lead poisoning, seizures, asthma, and high cancer rates. Moss Point resident Linda Young says, "I have ten grandchildren and five of them are asthmatic, and they are in and out of the hospital all through the year." The situation has worsened since 2005, when Hurricane Katrina deposited tons of river-bottom sediment and sludge contaminated with dioxin and PCB (polychlorinated biphenyl) in Gulf coast communities. As Wilma Subra, an environmental chemist who has long studied these communities puts it, "Prior to Hurricane Katrina, only 5 percent of the community was healthy, now that 5 percent is ill."

This story features the Holy Spirit-inspired efforts of the Rev. Richard Young, of the Greater First Baptist Church of Escatawpa, to motivate town residents to rise up and challenge the nearby polluting industries. The sorry state of Moss Point and Escatawpa is a stunning example of environmental racism, in which poor people of color are asked to tolerate systemic pollution of their homes and workplaces in exchange for jobs in the very industries that are ruining their lives. "There has not been a lot of protest," says resident Jerry Walley, "because people are on the payroll of the industry." Or as

Rev. Young exclaims, "The only reason the plants are here is because they are in a poor, black, poverty-stricken neighborhood." An antitoxics prophet, Rev. Young wants to force the Pascagoula petroleum industry, along with local and national governmental bodies, to remediate the toxins in coastal neighborhoods, compensate residents for their material losses and health problems, and consider moving townspeople en masse to safer areas.

Poor Gulf Coast communities are not alone in their struggles. The 1970s conflict at Love Canal, New York, is the first and best-known example of a modern successful grassroots response to callous irresponsibility on the part of the powerful industrial waste industry. A citizens' movement led by Love Canal homeowner-activist Lois Gibbs protested Hooker Chemical's disposal of toxic chemicals into the ground on which homes and schools were later built. The Love Canal homeowners convincingly documented the deleterious health effects that had resulted from living in the middle of a chemical dump and persuaded officials to buy out and permanently relocate town residents. Other recent local antitoxics campaigns are also notable, if not always as successful: the protest against siting a PCB landfill in Warren County, North Carolina; the movement against building a waste incinerator by the Mothers of East Los Angeles; the campaign by Native American activists against building a waste-to-fertilizer plant on Native lands in Vian, Oklahoma; and the ongoing resistance to petrochemical waste in Cancer Alley along the Mississippi River near Baton Rouge, Louisiana. Today, Rev. Young and residents of Moss Point and Escatawpa plan to take their David vs. Goliath fight to the state capital to persuade lawmakers to stop the environmental carnage in their respective communities as well.

Questions

1. Today's religious environmental movement high-
lights ecojustice as central to its mission. Ecojustice, as
the participants of the First National People of Color
Environmental Leadership Summit put it, "affirms the
sacredness of Mother Earth, ecological unity and the
interdependence of all species, and the right to be free
from ecological destruction." All persons are fundamentally equal and everyone has the right to family stability
and meaningful work in a healthy environment regardless of one's racial, cultural, economic, or sexual identity. But many poor persons—and especially minority
individuals—suffer disproportionate exposure to environmental hazards from industrial processing and waste
facilities. What, therefore, should the faith community's
response be to the specter of environmental racism in
towns like Moss Point and Escatawpa? Rev. Young seeks
to influence local and state officials to remediate the
toxics problem in his area through moral suasion. What
other direct-action tactics—for example, consumer boy-
cotting and class-action suits—could or should critics
employ to advance their aims?

2. What role should the Holy Spirit play in the religious
environmental movement? Throughout the history of
Christian resistance to cultural and political repression,
the Spirit has been invoked to lead the charge against
oppressive social institutions. In this regard, take note
of Spirit-centered movements for change in Christian
history: Thomas Müntzer's radical reformation, George
Fox's founding of Quakerism, abolitionists' attack on
slavery, and John Muir's fight to preserve Yosemite.

Rev. Young's antitoxics leadership is animated by the
presence and power of the Spirit in his life and ministry. "All of a sudden, out of nowhere," he says, "I heard
the Holy Spirit, and the Holy Spirit spoke to me to
call for a [chemical contamination] test of this environment." The Spirit, he announces, led him to understand
that "the general public was breathing death and didn't
know it!" For many faith communities, Spirit vocabulary and imagery has deep ecumenical resonances.
What role should language about and symbols of the
Spirit play in today's emerging religious environmental
movement?

Resources

Gottlieb, Robert. *Forcing the Spring: the Transformation of the
American Environmental Movement.* Washington, D.C.:
Island, 1993.

Martin-Schramm, James B., and Robert L. Stivers. *Christian
Environmental Ethics: A Case Method Approach.* Maryknoll, N.Y.: Orbis, 2003.

National Council of Churches Eco-Justice Program. www
.nccecojustice.org.

Rauschenbusch, Walter. *Christianity and the Social Crisis in the
21st Century.* Edited by Paul Rauschenbusch. New York:
HarperOne, 2007.

Taylor, Bron Raymond, ed. *Ecological Resistance Movements:
The Global Emergence of Radical and Popular Environmentalism.* New York: SUNY, 1995.

United Church of Christ, "Statements by United Church of
Christ on Environmental Racism in St. Louis." In *This Sacred*

Earth: Religion, Nature, Environment, edited by Roger S. Gottlieb, 712-15. 2nd ed. New York: Routledge, 2004.

Wallace, Mark I. "The Spirit of Environmental Justice: Resurrection Hope in Urban America," *Worldviews: Global Religions, Culture, and Ecology* 12 (2008): 255-69.

7. Sacred Celebration

Narrative

The orienting vision that animates *Renewal* is captured in this episode: the marriage of religion and social action to save the verdant gift of creation. Here we see how the "trendy development," as farmer John Shipley puts it, in the South Valley of Albuquerque, New Mexico, is destroying agricultural land and the way of life that it supports. This area relies on the *asecias* culture—an integrated ditch system that uses water from the Rio Grande to irrigate small-scale, often family-based farms. The *asecia* system is threatened by private property land claims that supersede communal water-sharing practices that have their origins in pre-white contact New Mexico. In response, Shipley; Joan Brown, a Franciscan sister; Albino Garcia, an Apache and Mexican Indian activist; and other Anglo, Latino, and Native American residents of the South Valley are pushing back against city officials and developers who see land as marketable commodity rather than sacred gift.

Central to residents' struggle is the recovery of land-based rituals within their own traditions—Christian and Native American, respectively—as necessary for emotionally grounding their ongoing fight to save the South Valley from market-based exploitation. As Joan Brown says, "Rituals have a way of engaging the whole person; we are touched on deeper levels; rituals move us in our hearts and spirits to protect [land and water]." Together, Sister Joan revitalizes a Catholic festival devoted to San Ysidro and Maria de la Cabesa, patron saints of agriculture, along with Albino Garcia's indigenous dance exercise in "offering prayers and ceremonies to the elements." These two rituals then blend together in a green tapestry of invocations, flower petals, drumming, singing and dancing that energizes South Valley residents to forcefully and compassionately persuade city officials to stop the encroaching development in their communities. This story is a multiracial and interfaith celebration of the potential of religious community to ground and empower the struggle for ecojustice in the face of threats to land, water, and food production basic to healthy, local living.

Questions

1. In much traditional Christianity, only God is worthy of devotion and praise; to accord the earth such honor, by implication, is a type of heathenism or idolatry that dare not speak its name. In this story, Albino Garcia talks about "water as the blood of Mother Earth"; similarly, Joan Brown discusses "blessing of seeds and harvest" as central to the San Ysidro celebration in the South Valley. These expressions are consistent with the mindset embodied in a recent cover article from *E: The Environmental Magazine* subtitled, "Why We Should All Worship the Ground We Walk On." The article implies that soil is worthy of our respect, even our adoration and reverence, because it is foundational to the life-sustaining ecosystems we all rely on for daily sustenance.

We should worship, as it were, the ground we walk on because it is basic to planetary well-being. At a time when the modern environmental movement, and religious leaders like Albino Garcia and Joan Brown are attaching spiritual significance to land and water, should Christians and other people of Abrahamic faith be troubled by the ascription of sacredness and blessing to anything other than God? Is Earth-based spirituality at the center of authentic religious faith, Christian or otherwise, or is it too closely allied with pagan sensibilities, and thereby an opening to ideas foreign to the historic monotheistic traditions?

2. How important is ritual to social change? Similar to Question 2 in the Compassion in Action story, the question that calls out for a response in this episode centers around the place of mindful, bodily activity (in this case, the San Ysidro celebration) as the basis for engaged social action with practical environmental consequences. "The practice of ritual and worship," according to John Shipley, "is in essence the way we prepare ourselves in the struggle we will have to fight." As we saw with the place of meditation in the Green Sangha's struggle against nonsustainable magazine production, is the use of ritual—or what some call *soulcraft*—as foundational to sustained justice-seeking work one of the distinctive contributions religion can make to the environmental movement?

Resources

Columbia River Pastoral Letter by the Catholic Bishops. www
.columbiariver.org.

Dunlap, Thomas R. *Faith in Nature: Environmentalism as Religious Quest*. Seattle: University of Washington Press, 2004.

Edwards, Denis. *Ecology at the Heart of Faith: The Change of Heart that Leads to a New Way of Living on Earth*. Maryknoll, N.Y.: Orbis, 2006.

Hart, John. *What are they Saying about Environmental Theology?* New York: Paulist, 2004.

Moseley, Lyndsay, ed. *Holy Ground: A Gathering of Voices on Caring for Creation*. San Francisco: Sierra Club Books, 2008.

Taylor, Sarah McFarland. *Green Sisters: A Spiritual Ecology*. Cambridge, Mass.: Harvard University Press, 2007.

Tinker, George E. *Spirit and Resistance: Political Theology and American Indian Liberation*. Minneapolis: Fortress Press, 2004.

8. Interfaith Power and Light

Narrative

A sermon about climate change from the Rev. Sally Bingham begins this segment: "Global warming is one-if not the most-serious moral issues of our time; each one of us has a role in keeping the planet safe and healthy." If the current scientific consensus is accurate, we are living in an objectively apocalyptic situation in which our planet is teetering on the edge of disaster. As we have seen, global warming is the trapping in Earth's atmosphere of greenhouse gases, such as CO_2 from car and power plant emissions, which is causing air and ocean temperatures to rise, ice caps to melt, and the seas to warm and rise.

Sally Bingham and her allies are rallying people of faith to confront this challenge by pushing legislators to pass laws that support renewable energy and enact mandatory greenhouse gas emissions caps. Interfaith Power and Light (IPL) is the organizational name of this effort in twenty-three states. On the one hand, IPL is a lobbing group that works with elected officials to enact climate-friendly legislation for a warming planet. On the other, it is a grassroots effort to motivate power companies and consumers to come together around sustainable living. In Atlanta, for example, Georgia Power contributed 3,500 compact fluorescent light bulbs for installation in public housing units in partnership with Antioch Baptist Church North. This effort "prevents 1,200 tons of CO_2 from escaping into the atmosphere," according to Rev. Woody Bartlett, who is aiding this utility-church partnership.

IPL is a multi-constituency, interfaith effort. The story ends with Rabbi Andrea Cohen-Kiener leading attendees at a national IPL meeting in singing a group harmony to prepare them for their creation-saving efforts when they return from the meeting to their respective home-state IPL chapters. The sing-along represents citizens from all walks of life and a variety of religious traditions. "What gives me hope," says Rabbi Cohen-Kiener, "is that I have never seen a wider coalition on any issue among faith communities; we have Jews sitting with Muslims and Episcopalians with Evangelicals; when so many of us have come together to find common ground there is hope." Religious faith has the distinctive power to gather together the fragments of human vision for a just and sustainable world into a coherent moral narrative that can enable the type of revolutionary social change needed in this historical moment. Precisely at this point in our history, when the Earth is most under siege, people of faith have become acutely aware of the life-giving ecological wisdom at the roots of the respective traditions. Finally, Christians and others are becoming awakened to their planetary responsibilities.

Questions

1. Should Christians today, and other people of faith, redefine their core values in terms of caring for creation? Is saving the planet essential to what it means to be religious in our time? In the eighteenth century, Quaker abolitionist John Woolman stopped wearing Indigo-dyed clothing because he discovered the link between West Indian slave dyers and the U.S. clothing industry. If slavery is a sin, reasoned Woolman, then consuming its byproducts is sinful as well. Similar to our questions about Big Coal in the first story, what are the "consumables" in our economy that are transgressions against God's will? "Episcopalians pray for a reverence for the Earth on Sunday," Sallie Bingham says, "and then people leave the church and drive away in a big SUV." Are we contributing to the destruction of Earth through our choices about goods and services? How is our market economy affecting the planet? And what better consumer choices can we make in order to reverse or blunt the coming storm of global warming?

2. This story shows members of the states' IPL lobbying members of Congress to promote climate justice legislation. Legislators take notice when large masses of people agitate for change. As Woody Bartlett puts it, "Politicians know clergy have influence over their congregations,

and we are starting to move a mass of people [toward creation care]." How should the religious community seek to influence elected officials around the issue of climate change? What are the opportunities and dangers for both groups—politicians and people of faith—when politics and religion are brought together in dialogue, disputation, and confrontation?

Resources

Abbasi, Daniel R. *Americans and Climate Change: Closing the Gap between Science and Action*. New Haven, Conn.: Yale School of Forestry and Environmental Studies, 2005.

Gore, Al. *An Inconvenient Truth: The Planetary Emergence of Global Warming and What We Can Do about It*. Emmaus, Penn.: Rodale, 2006.

Interfaith Power and Light. www.theregenerationproject.org

International Day of Climate Action, 24 October 2009. www.350.org.

McFague, Sallie. *A New Climate for Theology: God, the World, and Global Warming*. Minneapolis: Fortress, 2008.

McKibben, Bill. *Fight Global Warming Now: The Handbook for Taking Action in Your Community*. New York: Henry Holt and Company, 2007.

Northcott, Michael S. *A Moral Climate: The Ethics of Global Warming*. New York: Orbis, 2007.

Pearce, Fred. *With Speed and Violence: Why Scientists Fear Tripping Points in Climate Change*. Boston: Beacon, 2007.

Primavesi, Anne. *Theology in a Time of Climate Change: Participating in the Wisdom of Gaia*. New York: Routledge, 2008.

Conclusion

The writing of this book has come at a difficult time in my life. Last month I divorced my wife of twenty-five years after a two-year separation. Ellen and I have two teenage children, Katie and Chris, so the ending of our marriage was heart-wrenching for us and for our children. This book came together over the final years of our partnership and separation, and I dedicate it to my recently broken but healing family—to the good faith and commitment to one another's well-being we have always sought to demonstrate to one another.

I now live in the well of memories through which my family sustained me over these past years. Many of these memories spring from signal events when love of nature and care of our bodies defined our life together. One reminiscence stems from a time when our home became surrounded by summer-nesting birds that blocked the entryway through our front door. While we were away on vacation, a pair of Carolina Wrens made a nest in a hanging flower basket just to the side of the front door. Wrens are well known for finding almost any available object as a nesting site: mailboxes, tin cans, old shoes, hats, teapots, and clothes left on a clothesline. In this case, a hanging basket was the preferred option for creating a nest cavity in the soft dirt of the basket. The parent birds spent much of the day foraging for grubs and worms to bring back to the nest, while two fledglings lived deep in the hallowed out hole in the flower basket. The parents' teakettle call announced their approach and sent the baby birds into a frenzy of shaking, with beaks frantically wide open as they anticipated their meal. Ellen, Katie, Chris, and I crept back and forth across our front porch that summer in order not to disturb this fragile ecology. We were afraid that if we became too visible around the hanging basket, the parent wrens might abandon the nest and leave the fledglings to fend for themselves.

On this and many occasions, we were our own green team: a family working together to protect the much beloved habitat of our avian friends. Carrying this poignant memory in my heart, I am daily renewed in my desire to join again in the great song of creation to love all flesh as the wrens loved their nestlings, as God loves us. May we all be empowered to do likewise.

NOTES

Chapter 1: Find God Everywhere

1. Native American Prayer, "Now Talking God," in *Earth Prayers: From Around the World, 365 Prayers, Poems, and Invocations for Honoring the Earth*, ed. Elizabeth Roberts and Elias Amidon (San Francisco: HarperSanFrancisco, 1991) 32.

2. Henry David Thoreau, "Walking," in *The Norton Book of American Nature Writing*, ed. John Elder and Robert Finch (New York: W. W. Norton, 1990) 183.

3. The sensibility here is borrowed from Friedrich Hölderlin by way of Martin Heidegger and Paul Ricoeur. Hölderlin writes that "Full of merit, and yet poetically, dwells man on this earth" (quoted in Paul Ricoeur, "Religion, Atheism, and Faith," in *The Conflict of Interpretations* [Evanston, Ill.: Northwestern University Press, 1974] 466–67). Poetry is a meaning-making activity that invests life with a measure of coherence, even purpose. Language is a world-creating exercise that converts existence in empty space into habitation or "dwelling," in Hölderlin's parlance, in a world charged with rich possibilities.

4. Graham Harvey, "Animism—A Contemporary Perspective," in *The Encyclopedia of Religion and Nature*, eds. Bron R. Taylor et al., 2 vols. (New York: Continuum, 2005) 1:81.

5. "Pseudo-Titus," in Bart D. Ehrman, *Lost Christianities: Books That Did Not Make It into the New Testament* (Oxford: Oxford University Press, 2003) 239.

6. Sallie McFague, *The Body of God: An Ecological Theology* (Minneapolis: Fortress, 1993) 149–50.

7. "The Creed of Chalcedon," in Philip Schaff, ed., *The Creeds of Christendom*, 3 vols. (Grand Rapids, Mich.: Baker Book House, 1983) 2:62.

8. See Martin Buber, *The Eclipse of God: Studies in the Relation between Religion and Philosophy* (New York: Humanity Books, 1988).

9. Jim Hansen, quoted in Bill McKibben, "Global Warming," *Salon.com* (22 February 2007).

10. See full report at www.ipcc.ch.

11. Elisabeth Rosenthal and Andrew C. Revkin, "Science Panel Says Global Warming is 'Unequivocal,'" *The New York Times* (3 February 2007) A1, A5. Also see James Gustave Speth, *Red Sky at Morning: America and the Crisis of the Global Environment* (New Haven: Yale University Press, 2004); and Elizabeth Kolbert, *Field Notes from a Catastrophe: Man, Nature, and Climate Change* (New York: Bloomsbury, 2006).

12. I recently partnered with a group of students at Swarthmore College to found a twelve-step group called "Carbon Addicts Anonymous." Using Web-based carbon calculators, we measured our individual carbon output and developed lifestyle changes to reduce our output. This effort has given me hope that small groups of committed individuals can band together to reduce significantly their discharge of fossil fuel waste and thereby save the planet, at least for human habitation.

13. The fault lines over climate change and related issues within the former president's religious base first caught my attention in 2005. In May of that year Mr. Bush delivered the commencement address at Calvin College, a conservative Christian

liberal arts college in Grand Rapids, Michigan. Some 140 members of the college' faculty and staff signed an open letter denouncing the president's policies on everything from the war in Iraq to bad stewardship of the environment. For text of the letter, visit www .commondreams.org/views05/0520-27.htm. In 2006, and in opposition to some of their colleagues, a significant group of Christian conservatives signed the Evangelical Climate Initiative. The statement says that faith in Jesus compels Christians to love their neighbors, especially the most vulnerable among us, and that the global poor will be disproportionately affected by the flooding, famine, and political instability that climate change is certain to produce. The statement is also a call to action: Christians should pressure their federal legislators to implement legally binding carbon dioxide emissions caps to blunt the effects of continuing climate change. For text visit www.christiansandclimate.org.

14. For an analysis of the relationship between apocalyptic theology and environmentalism, see Stephenie Hendricks, *Divine Destruction: Wise Use, Dominion Theology, and the Making of American Environmental Policy* (Hoboken, N.J.: Melville, 2005); and Bill Moyers, *Welcome to Doomsday* (New York: New York Review Book, 2006).

15. J. Matthew Sleeth, *Serve God, Save the Planet: A Christian Call to Action* (White River Junction, Vt.: Chelsea Green, 2006) 10.

16. David D. Kirkpatrick, "End Times for Evangelicals?" *The New York Times Magazine* (28 October 2007) 60.

17. Matthew Sleeth, "How Evangelicals View the Future," *Creation Care* 34 (Fall 2007): 24–25.

18. For an excellent overview of how institutional and grassroots religious communities are facing the environmental crisis, see Roger Gottlieb, *A Greener Faith: Religious Environmentalism and Our Planet's Future* (New York: Oxford University Press, 2006). An inspiring feature-length documentary of the growing religious environmental movement is *Renewal*, produced and directed by Marty Ostrow and Terry Kay Rockefeller. A DVD copy is included here, and www.renewalproject.net. This film is also the focus of chapter 6.

19. See Norman C. Habel, *Seven Songs of Creation: Liturgies for Celebrating and Healing Earth* (Cleveland: Pilgrim, 2004).

20. Susan Gilbert Zencka, "The Web of Creation and Dollar Stores," unpublished sermon, September 30, 2007.

21. Tamsyn Jones, "The Scoop on Dirt: Why We Should All Worship the Ground We Walk On," *E: The Environmental Magazine* (September-October 2006) 26–39.

22. Lester Brown, quoted in Jeanne Roy, *Ten Stresses on the Planet* (Portland: Center for Earth Leadership, 2008) 11.

23. Thomas Berry, *The Great Work: Our Way into the Future* (New York: Bell Tower, 1999) 7.

24. The seventh-generation ideal is also identified today as the *triple bottom line business model* (people, planet, profit). In this model, financial profits depend upon carefully managed environmental and social performance. Here corporate, societal, and ecological interests dynamically interact and mutually support one another. This model is analyzed as the "new bottom line" in Michael Lerner, *The Left Hand of God: Taking Back Our Country from the Religious Right* (San Francisco: HarperSanFrancisco, 2006) 227–40; as "oikonomia economics" in Herman E. Daly and John B. Cobb, Jr., *For the Common Good: Redirecting the Economy toward Community, the Environment, and a Sustainable Future*, 2d. ed. (Boston: Beacon, 1989, 1994) 138–75; and "ecologically reformed capitalism" in Gottlieb, *A Greener Faith*, 81–110.

Chapter 2: Read the Bible with Green Eyes

1. Norman C. Habel, "Introducing the Earth Bible," in *Readings from the Perspective of Earth,* ed. Habel, vol. 1 of *The Earth Bible* (Sheffield, England: Sheffield, 2000) 35. The five volumes of *The Earth Bible,* edited variously by Norman C. Habel, Shirley Wurst, and Vicky Balabanski from 2000 to 2002 set the standard for a systematic reinterpretation of the Bible as an "earthen vessel." Similarly, see Barbara R. Rossing, *The Rapture Exposed: The Message of Hope in the Book of Revelation* (New York: Basic, 2004); and H. Paul Santmire, *Nature Reborn: The Ecological and*

Cosmic Promise of Christian Theology (Minneapolis: Fortress, 2000), esp. 29–44.

2. See Hans-Georg Gadamer, *Truth and Method*, trans. Garrett Barden and John Cumming (New York: Continuum, 1975), esp. 235–344, and Paul Ricoeur, "Naming God," in *Figuring the Sacred: Religion, Narrative, and Imagination*, ed. Mark I. Wallace, trans. David Pellauer (Minneapolis: Fortress, 1995) 217–35.

3. Herod Antipas was the son of the notorious Herod the Great, who slaughtered the male children of Bethlehem during Jesus' infancy in order to destroy the long-promised baby messiah, according to Matthew. Jesus was fully aware of the danger of crossing the Herod family. Like his father, Herod Antipas, learning of Jesus' growing influence, decided that Jesus must be put to death—presumably completing the work his murderous father was unable to accomplish.

4. Neil Darragh, quoted in Denis Edwards, *Ecology at the Heart of Faith: The Change of Heart That Leads to a New Way of Living on Earth* (Maryknoll, N.Y.: Orbis, 2006) 58–60. In addition to this book and Edwards's *Jesus the Wisdom of God: An Ecological Theology* (Maryknoll, N.Y.: Orbis, 1995), other ecological christologies include Sallie McFague, *The Body of God: An Ecological Theology* (Minneapolis: Fortress, 1993); J. Matthew Sleeth, *Serve God, Save the Planet: A Christian Call to Action* (White River Junction, Vt.: Chelsea Green, 2006); James Jones, *Jesus and the Earth* (Kelowna, B.C.: Wood Lake, 2003); and James B. Martin-Schramm and Robert L. Stivers, *Christian Environmental Ethics: A Case Method Approach* (Maryknoll, N.Y.: Orbis, 2003).

5. On the new poor, see McFague, *The Body of God* 165-78.

6. I am grateful to Patrick Keifert for the reminder that Jesus' aesthetic passion for nonhuman nature is one of the wellsprings that feeds his moral convictions about responsible Earth care.

7. Thich Nhat Hanh, *Living Buddha, Living Christ* (New York: Riverhead, 1995) 21.

8. The emerging field of eco-pneumatology—nature-based reconstructions of the doctrine of the Holy Spirit—is represented by the work of Sharon Betcher, *Spirit and the Politics of*

Disablement (Minneapolis: Fortress Press, 2007); Chung Hyun-
Kyung, "Welcome the Spirit; Hear Her Cries: The Holy Spirit, Creation, and the Culture of Life," *Christianity and Crisis* 51 (July
15, 1991) 220–23; Catherine Keller, *Face of the Deep: A Theology
of Becoming* (London: Routledge, 2003); Jürgen Moltmann, *God
in Creation: A New Theology of Creation and the Spirit of God*,
trans. Margaret Kohl (Minneapolis: Fortress Press, 1993); *idem*,
The Source of Life: The Holy Spirit and the Theology of Life, trans.
Margaret Kohl (Minneapolis: Fortress Press, 1997); Geiko Müller-
Fahrenholz, *God's Spirit: Transforming a World in Crisis*, trans.
John Cumming (New York: Continuum, 1995); Nancy Victorin
Vangerud, *The Raging Hearth: Spirit in the Household of God* (St.
Louis: Chalice Press, 2000); Mark I. Wallace, *Finding God in the
Singing River: Christianity, Spirit, Nature* (Minneapolis: Fortress
Press, 2005); and Michael Welker, *God the Spirit*, trans. John F.
Hoffmeyer (Minneapolis: Fortress Press, 1994).

9. On the biblical and theological history of feminine lan-
guage and imagery for the Spirit, see Susan Ashbrook Harvey,
"Feminine Imagery for the Divine: The Holy Spirit, the Odes of
Solomon, and Early Syriac Tradition," *Saint Vladimir's Theologi-
cal Quarterly* 37 (1993) 111–40; Gary Steven Kinkel, *Our Dear
Mother the Spirit: An Investigation of Count Zinzendorf's Theology
and Praxis* (Lanham, Md.: University Press of America, 1990); and
Elizabeth A. Johnson, *She Who Is: The Mystery of God in Feminist
Theological Discourse* (New York: Crossroad, 1992), especially
128–31.

10. Ellen Armour, "Toward an Elemental Theology," in *Theology That Matters*, ed. Darby Kathleen Ray (Minneapolis: Fortress,
2006) 54.

Chapter 3: Enjoy the Flesh

1. See Mark D. Jordan, *The Ethics of Sex* (Oxford: Blackwell,
2002); Stephanie Paulsell, *Honoring the Body: Meditations on a
Christian Practice* (San Francisco: Jossey-Bass, 2002); Eugene F.
Rogers, Jr., ed., *Theology and Sexuality: Classic and Contemporary*

Readings (Oxford: Blackwell, 2002); and Virginia Burrus and Catherine Keller, eds., *Toward a Theology of Eros: Transfiguring Passion at the Limits of Discipline* (Fordham: Fordham University Press, 2006).

2. My convention regarding S/spirit: when referring to the Spirit of God (e.g., the Holy Spirit) I generally use the definite article and capitalize this word, whereas when referring to the innermost aspect of a person or place (e.g., the "spirit of Christianity" or the "spirit of Rome") I put the first letter of this word into lower case.

3. Daniel Boyarin, *Carnal Israel: Reading Sex in Talmudic Culture* (Berkeley: University of California Press, 1993) 6 n.11.

4. Peter Brown, *The Body and Society: Men, Women, and Sexual Renunciation in Early Christianity* (New York: Columbia University Press, 1988) 160–89.

5. Jordan, *Ethics of Sex,* 48.

6. But see the early Syriac body-affirming alternative to the antibody sensibility in Pseudo-Titus and similar canonical and extracanonical texts, in Susan A. Harvey, "Embodiment in Time and Eternity: A Syriac Perspective," in Rogers, ed., *Theology and Sexuality,* 3–22.

7. "Pseudo-Titus," in Bart Ehrman, ed., *Lost Scriptures: Books That Did Not Make It into the New Testament* (Oxford: Oxford University Press, 2003) 246.

8. Augustine, *City of God,* trans. Marcus Dods (New York: Modern Library, 2000) 13, 14.

9. Elaine Pagels, *Adam, Eve, and the Serpent: Sex and Politics in Early Christianity* (New York: Random House, 1988) 109.

10. Ibid., 111.

11. Clayton Sullivan, *Rescuing Sex from the Christians* (New York: Continuum, 2006) 32–33.

12. See I. Howard Marshall, *The Gospel of Luke: A Commentary on the Greek Text* (Grand Rapids, Mich.: Eerdmans, 1978) 304–14.

13. On the importance of feminist critique in biblical studies, see Margaret D. Kamitsuka, "Toward a Feminist Postmodern and Postcolonial Interpretation of Sin," *Journal of Religion* 84 (January 2004) 179–211; Wonhee Anne Joh, *Heart of the Cross: A Postcolonial Christology* (Louisville, Ky.: Westminster John Knox, 2006); and Kwok Pui-lan, *Postcolonial Imagination and Feminist Theology* (Louisville, Ky.: Westminster John Knox, 2006).

14. The argument for the anonymous Lukan woman as a prostitute is made by Elizabeth Schüssler Fiorenza, *In Memory of Her: A Feminist Theological Reconstruction of Christian Origins* (New York: Crossroad, 1984); and François Bovon, *Luke 1: A Commentary on the Gospel of Luke 1:1-9:50*, trans. Christine M. Thomas and ed. Helmut Koester (Minneapolis: Fortress, 2002) 293–96. Another perspective is found in Barbara E. Reid, " 'Do You See This Woman?': A Liberative Look at Luke 7.36–50 and Strategies for Reading Other Lukan Stories against the Grain," in Amy-Jill Levine, ed., *A Feminist Companion to Luke* (Cleveland: Pilgrim, 2001) 106–20, and Teresa J. Hornsby, "The Woman Is a Sinner/The Sinner Is a Woman," in Levine, *A Feminist Companion to Luke*, 121–32.

15. See Gail Corrington Streete, *The Strange Woman: Power and Sex in the Bible* (Louisville, Ky.: Westminster John Knox, 1997); and Carla Ricci, *Mary Magdalene and Many Others: Women Who Followed Jesus*, trans. Paul Burns (Minneapolis: Fortress, 1994).

16. Of course, so much more could be said about Mary Magdalene than what I have space for here. We know that Mary was very close to Jesus, but how close? On Easter morning, e.g., does she go to the tomb in the dark to sit with her friend, or her lover? Some exegetes argue that Mary and Jesus regularly touched one another, perhaps sexually (so Jesus to Mary in John 20:17, "Do not hold me, do not touch me"). This question is sharpened by the portrait of the extracanonical Gnostic Mary Magdalene, who has frequent visions of Christ in which she is identified as his lover and partner, perhaps even his spouse: "The consort of Christ is Mary Magdalene. The Lord loved Mary more than all the disciples and he kissed her on the mouth many times. The others

said to him, 'Why do you love her more than all of us?' " ("Gospel of Philip," in Ehrman, ed., *Lost Scriptures: Books That Did Not Make It into the New Testament*, 42.)

17. See Bovon, *Luke 1*, 291.

18. Anne F. Elvey, *An Ecological Feminist Reading of the Gospel of Luke: A Gestational Paradigm* (Lewiston, N.Y.: Edwin Mellen, 2005) 214.

19. Bovon, *Luke 1*, 295.

20. Teresa J. Hornsby, "The Woman Is a Sinner," in Levine, *A Feminist Companion to Luke* 122–23.

21. For other such titles for this passage, see Reid, 'Do You See This Woman?' 112.

22. In consulting similar Bibles and titles for this section, I was not able to find any that spoke directly to the woman's great love for Jesus.

23. See D. Harvey, "Book of Ruth," in George Arthur Buttrick, ed., *The Interpreter's Dictionary of the Bible*, 4 vols. (Nashville: Abingdon, 1962) 4:131–34.

24. In this regard see Amy-Jill Levine, "Ruth," in Carol A. Newsom and Sharon H. Ringe, eds., *The Women's Bible Commentary* (Louisville: Westminster John Knox, 1992) 78–84.

25. See B. L. Bandstra and A. D. Verhey, "Sex: sexuality," in Geoffrey W. Bromiley, ed., *The International Standard Bible Encyclopedia* (Grand Rapids, Mich.: Eerdmans, 1988) 430–35.

26. Hornsby, "The Woman Is a Sinner," 129.

27. Valerie Smith, " 'Circling the Subject': History and Narrative in *Beloved*," in Henry Louis Gates, Jr., and K. A. Appiah, eds., *Toni Morrison: Critical Perspectives Past and Present* (New York: Amistad, 1993) 346.

28. Toni Morrison, *Beloved* (New York: Knopf, 1987) 88.

29. Barbara Christian, "Fixing Methodologies: *Beloved*," *Cultural Critique* 25 (1993) 14–15.

30. Morrison, *Beloved*, 17.

31. Morrison, *Beloved*, 17–18.

32. See Friedrich Nietzsche, *The Genealogy of Morals*, trans. Douglas Smith (Oxford: Oxford University Press, 1996).

Chapter 4: Eat Well (Seek Justice)

1. Thich Nhat Hanh, "Earth Gathas," in *This Sacred Earth: Religion, Nature, Environment,* ed. Roger S. Gottlieb, 2d ed. (New York: Routledge, 2004) 515.

2. For more information about the Chester Community Grocery Co-op, go to www.chestercoop.com.

3. Gary W. Fick, *Food, Farming, and Faith* (New York: SUNY Press, 2008) 129.

4. See Elizabeth McLean Petras, "From Paternalism to Patronage to Pillage: Chester, Pa., A Chronicle of the Embedded Consciousness of Place in the Second Most Economically Depressed City in the U.S.," unpublished paper delivered at the North Central Sociological Annual Meeting, Dearborn, Mich. (April 25-28, 1991) 1–34, and Jeff Gammage, "The Ball's in Chester's Court," *Philadelphia Inquirer* (January 7, 2008) A1, A7.

5. For reproductions and story about the Chester mural, go to www.sccs.swarthmore.edu/org/cmc. The mural is copyright © Swarthmore College.

6. Jürgen Moltmann, *Theology of Hope: On the Ground and the Implications of a Christian Eschatology,* trans. James W. Leitch (Minneapolis: Fortress Press, 1991 [1967]) 338.

7. See Frederick Douglass, *Narrative of the Life of Frederick Douglass* (New York: Signet, 2005).

8. See Obery M. Hendricks, Jr., *The Politics of Jesus: Rediscovering the True Revolutionary Nature of Jesus' Teachings and How They Have Been Corrupted* (New York: Doubleday, 2006).

9. See Petras, "From Paternalism to Patronage to Pillage," 25; and Gregory L. Volz. "Making Chester Work—Now," unpublished report of the Community Economic Development Resource Center (2005) 1–59.

10. See James Gardner Colins, "Commonwealth of Pennsylvania, Department of Education, Petitioner v. Chester-Upland School District Special Board of Control" (Philadelphia: Commonwealth Court of Pennsylvania, 2006) 44–45.

11. Gloria Grantham, quoted in Colins, "Commonwealth of Pennsylvania," 45.

12. See Mark I. Wallace, *Finding God in the Singing River: Christianity, Spirit, Nature* (Minneapolis: Fortress, 2005) 57–80; Chester Residents Concerned for Quality Living, "Pollution and Industry in Chester's 'West End,'" pamphlet, 1996; Luke Cole and Sheila R. Foster, *From the Ground Up: Environmental Racism and the Rise of the Environmental Justice Movement* (New York: New York University Press, 2001); and Bob Edwards, "With Liberty and Environmental Justice for All: The Emergence and Challenge of Grassroots Environmentalism in the United States," in Bron Raymond Taylor, ed., *Ecological Resistance Movements: The Global Emergence of Radical and Popular Environmentalism* (Albany: State University of New York Press, 1995) 35–55.

13. Maryanne Voller, "Everyone Has Got to Breathe," *Audubon* (March–April 1995); and Cole and Foster, *From the Ground Up.*

14. Barbara Bohannan-Sheppard, "Remarks," *Department of Environmental Resources Public Hearing,* transcript (February 17, 1994); also see the video produced by Robert Bahar and George McCullough, "Laid to Waste: A Chester Neighborhood Fights for Its Future," (Berkeley, Calif.: University of California Extension Center for Media and Independent Learning, 1996).

15. Will Richan, "Time to Invest in Chester's Human Capital," *Delaware County Daily Times* (July 30, 2007) 22.

16. Fair Deal Coalition, "Rolling the Dice: Gambling with Chester's Future." http://www.fairdealchester.org 2006.

17. Tracey L. Farrigan, *Sin or Savior? Weighing the Poverty and Social Impacts of Casino Development,* Ph.D. dissertation (Collegeville, Penn.: Pennsylvania State University, 2005).

18. "Ohio Public Health Association on Obesity." http://www.ohiopha.org/Member/Obesity/index.htm (2008).

19. Adam Drewnowski and S. E. Specter, "Poverty and Obesity: The Role of Energy Density and Energy Costs," *American Journal of Clinical Nutrition* 79 (2004) 6–16; and Lynn E. Kelly and Barbara J. Patterson, "Childhood Nutrition: Perceptions of Caretakers in a Low-Income Urban Setting," *Journal of School Nursing* 22 (2006): 345–51.

20. Benjamin Caballero, "The Global Epidemic of Obesity: An Overview," *Epidemiologic Reviews* 29 (2007) 1–5.

21. Herman Daly and John B. Cobb, Jr., *For the Common Good: Redirecting the Economy toward Community, the Environment, and a Sustainable Future*, 2d ed., (Boston: Beacon, 1994).

Chapter 5: Live a Vocation

1. Andrew W. Savitz with Karl Weber, The Triple Bottom Line: How Today's Best-Run Companies Are Achieving Economic, Social, and Environmental Success—and How You Can Too (Francisco: Jossey-Bass, 2006) x.

2. Paul Ricoeur, *Oneself as Another,* trans. Kathleen Blamey (Chicago: University of Chicago Press, 1992) 179.

3. Paul Ricoeur, *Oneself as Another,* 172.

4. Fred Pearce, With Speed and Violence: Why Scientists Fear Tipping Points in Climate Change (Boston: Beacon, 2008) xxviii.

5. Nicholas Schmidle, "Wanted: A New Home for My Country," *The New York Times Magazine,* 10 May 2009: 38–43.

6. "Cornwall Declaration," 2008. http://www.acton.org/ppolicy/environment/cornwall.php

7. See James Gustave Speth, *Red Sky at Morning: America and the Crisis of the Global Environment* (New Haven: Yale University Press, 2004).

8. Herman Daly and John B. Cobb, Jr., *For the Common Good: Redirecting the Economy toward Community, the Environment, and a Sustainable Future*, 2d ed. (Boston: Beacon, 1994).

9. Savitz with Weber, *The Triple Bottom Line,* x-xi.

10. See Bill McKibben, *Deep Economy: The Wealth of Communities and the Durable Future* (New York: Henry Holt and Company, 2007); Paul Hawken, *The Ecology of Commerce: A Declaration of Sustainability* (New York: HarperBusiness, 1993); and Savitz with Weber, *The Triple Bottom Line.*

11. David Specht and Richard Broholm, *Toward a Theology of Institutions* (Indianapolis: Greenleaf Center for Servant-Leadership, 2003).

12. John Todd and Nancy Jack Todd, "Living Machines," in *Steering Business toward Sustainability*, eds. Fritjof Capra and Gunter Pauli (Tokyo: United Nations University Press, 1995) 164.

13. Ibid.

14. Parker J. Palmer, *Let Your Life Speak: Listening for the Voice of Vocation* (San Francisco: Jossey-Bass, 2000) 44.

15. Dietrich Bonhoeffer, *The Cost of Discipleship*, trans. John W. de Gruchy (London: SCM, 1949) 99.

16. Dietrich Bonhoeffer, *Ethics*, trans. Neville Horton Smith and ed. Eberhard Bethge (New York: Macmillan, 1965) 339–53.

17. Ibid., 245.

18. Peter Senge, *The Fifth Discipline: The Art and Practice of the Learning Organization* (New York: Currency Doubleday, 1994) 159.

19. Søren Kierkegaard, *Fear and Trembling/Repetition*, trans. Howard V. and Edna H. Hong (Princeton: Princeton University Press, 1983) 36.

20. Robert K. Greenleaf, *Servant Leadership: A Journey into the Nature of Legitimate Power and Greatness* (New York: Paulist, 1977) 23.

21. Barack Obama, "A More Perfect Union." http://www.barackobama.com/2008/03/18/remarks_of_senator_barack_obama_53.php (accessed April 8, 2009).

22. Peter M. Senge, "The Leader's New Work: Building Learning Organizations," *Sloan Management Review* 32 (1990): 21.

23. In this regard, I am indebted to Margaret Benefiel and Kerry Hamilton, "Infinite Leadership: The Power of Spirit at Work," in *Spirituality in Business: Theory, Practice, and Future Directions*, eds. Jerry Biberman and Len Tischler (New York: Palgrave Macmillan, 2008) 141–59; and Tom Henry, "Landry's Bicycles and the Threefold Model" (Shelburne Falls, Mass.: Seeing Things Whole, 2006).

24. "Landry's Bicycles," Buyer's Guide (Natick, Mass., 2008).

25. "Landry's Bicycles." http://www.landrys.com.

26. Ibid.

27. Andrew Leonard, "A Battle Bush's EPA Can't Win," 2007. http://www.salon.com/tech/htww/2007/12/20/california_and_the_epa_2 (accessed April 8, 2009).

28. Sam Daley-Harris, ed., *Pathways Out of Poverty: Innovations in Microfinance for the Poorest Families* (Bloomfield, Conn.: Kumarian, 2002).

29. See Benefiel and Hamilton, "Infinite Leadership," 141–59.

30. Tom Henry, "Landry's Bicycles and the Threefold Model" (Shelburne Falls, Mass.: Seeing Things Whole, 2006) 2.

31. Ibid., 6.

32. "Bikes Belong." (http://www.bikesbelong.org).

33. Paul Hawken, *The Ecology of Commerce: A Declaration of Sustainability* (New York: HarperBusiness, 1993) 34.

34. Todd and Todd, "Living Machines," 163–77; and Hawken, *The Ecology of Commerce.*

35. Savitz with Weber, *The Triple Bottom Line,* 94.

36. Benefiel and Hamilton, "Infinite Leadership," 157–58.

37. Berry, *The Great Work,* 7.

INDEX

The DVD in this volume contains a video introduction to Green Christianity, *the author's brief introductions to the eight stories profiled in the final chapter, and brief video excerpts from the Renewal Project's acclaimed film about those initiatives.*

◊

"The religious environmental movement is potentially key to dealing with the greatest problem humans have ever faced, and it has never been captured with more breadth and force than in RENEWAL. I hope this movie is screened in church basements and synagogue social halls across the country, and that it moves many more people of faith off the fence and into action."—Bill McKibben

Special Offer

A complete DVD of
RENEWAL

*Stories from America's
Religious-Environmental Movement*

is available from the Renewal Project:
http://renewalproject.net/dvd
or by calling 617-354-2288

Individual copies, as well as discounts for multi-copy purchases, community/classroom licenses, and arrangements for educational and library sales are all available there.